Using and Interpreting Statistics in the Social, Behavioral, and Health Sciences

For Justin and Thomas

Using and Interpreting Statistics in the Social, Behavioral, and Health Sciences

William E. Wagner, III
California State University, Channel Islands

Brian Joseph Gillespie
Sonoma State University

Los Angeles | London | New Delhi
Singapore | Washington DC | Melbourne

FOR INFORMATION:

SAGE Publications, Inc.
2455 Teller Road
Thousand Oaks, California 91320
E-mail: order@sagepub.com

SAGE Publications Ltd.
1 Oliver's Yard
55 City Road
London, EC1Y 1SP
United Kingdom

SAGE Publications India Pvt. Ltd.
B 1/I 1 Mohan Cooperative Industrial Area
Mathura Road, New Delhi 110 044
India

SAGE Publications Asia-Pacific Pte. Ltd.
3 Church Street
#10-04 Samsung Hub
Singapore 049483

Printed in the United States of America

Library of Congress Cataloging-in-Publication Data

Names: Wagner, William E. (William Edward), author. | Gillespie, Brian Joseph, author.

Title: Using and interpreting statistics in the social, behavioral, and health sciences / William E. Wagner, California State University, Brian J. Gillespie, Sonoma State University, USA.

Description: First Edition. | Thousand Oaks : SAGE Publications, [2018]

Identifiers: LCCN 2017049830 | ISBN 9781526402493 (pbk. : alk. paper)

Subjects: LCSH: Statistics--Methodology. | Social sciences--Statistical methods. | Medical sciences--Statistical methods.

Classification: LCC HA29 .W3325 2018 | DDC 001.4/22--dc23 LC record available at https://lccn.loc.gov/2017049830

This book is printed on acid-free paper.

Acquisitions Editor: Jeff Lasser
Editorial Assistant: Tiara Beatty
Production Editor: Laureen Gleason
Copy Editor: Liann Lech
Typesetter: Hurix Digital
Proofreader: Wendy Jo Dymond
Cover Designer: Michael Dubowe
Marketing Manager: Kara Kindstrom

18 19 20 21 22 10 9 8 7 6 5 4 3 2 1

• Brief Contents •

• Detailed Contents •

• Acknowledgments •

Many thanks are due to Jeff Lasser at SAGE Publications for his support and guidance in the development of this book. We are also grateful for earlier guidance from both Vicki Knight and Jerry Westby, both now in retirement from SAGE Publications.

Sara Miller McCune founded SAGE Publishing in 1965 to support the dissemination of usable knowledge and educate a global community. SAGE publishes more than 1000 journals and over 800 new books each year, spanning a wide range of subject areas. Our growing selection of library products includes archives, data, case studies and video. SAGE remains majority owned by our founder and after her lifetime will become owned by a charitable trust that secures the company's continued independence.

Los Angeles | London | New Delhi | Singapore | Washington DC | Melbourne

Brief Introduction to Research in the Social, Behavioral, and Health Sciences

What Is the Purpose of Research?

Research is the process that informs us about scientific knowledge. How do we know things? Research is the mechanism that allows us to acquire and refine knowledge. It is undertaken in disciplines in the natural sciences, social sciences, health sciences, and beyond. Existing research is then used as a starting place for future research. In other words, we proceed from what we know from existing research and then use our own research to extend that further. Another way to think of it is that scientific research is like a conversation between scientists who contribute their findings to the literature and then continue communicating by conducting follow-up research that may bolster or contradict the original research, or may take the conversation (research literature) in a different direction altogether.

How Is Research Done?

Research is carried out using systematic and verifiable methods. Systematic methods are important so that bias can be minimized in research. Without implementing systematic methods, if you get two different results in two different experiments, it may well be that the methodology is the cause of the difference if the process wasn't carried out systematically. Moreover, it is extremely important to document your methodology as well as any difficulties, changes, and so on that occurred while you were conducting your research. This verifiable evidence allows you to demonstrate the efficacy of your findings, but beyond that, it will allow you or other researchers to better use data or findings from your study in the future as a starting block for subsequent research. Without those important details, it may be more difficult to understand the process that was used, which informs the process for future study.

Scientific Method and Hypothesis Testing

Almost all students learn something about the scientific method in science classes as early as elementary school. The key things that we learned then hold true in more advanced work as well. The scientific method allows us to eliminate alternative hypotheses, leaving our research hypothesis with greater credibility (rather than "proving" a particular research hypothesis).

In scientific research, you might think it would be appropriate to say that you proved something, but that is never the appropriate way to describe what happens in scientific research. It is not like a court of law where lawyers seek to prove something. As described below, you will see that in addition to your own hypothesis, you will state the opposite hypothesis, a statement of no difference where your hypothesis is the theory that is "different." At that point, the scientific research sets out to either "reject" the statement of no difference (the competing hypothesis), or it "fails to reject" that statement of no difference. If the statement of no difference is rejected, then that leaves your hypothesis standing as the remaining explanation, but we would not use the word *proved* to describe the result. If the scientific research fails to reject that statement of no difference, then this is an indicator that the statement of no difference could be right. You have not proved that either, but this situation does not provide any support for your hypothesis.

The scientific method we use is rooted in positivist philosophy, holding the assumption that there is such a thing as objective reality. The idea is that while we may not be able to directly see this "reality," we can directly observe measures that provide information about objective reality. This is the idea that underpins research methodology procedures.

Specific hypothesis tests are covered later in this book (see Chapter 8). The format of a hypothesis test can look something like this:

H_1: The research hypothesis

(the thing you think might be true)

H_0: The null hypothesis

(the thing that is a statement of no difference)

This will be discussed later in this book, but for now, here's what the hypothesis test might look like, using symbols and explained below:

H_1: The mean (of something) for Group 1 is greater than the mean for Group 2.

H_0: The mean (of something) for Group 1 is the same as the mean for Group 2.

In symbols:

H_1: $\mu_1 > \mu_2$

H_0: $\mu_1 = \mu_2$

where

μ_1 is the population mean of Group 1

μ_2 is the population mean of Group 2

(μ is the Greek letter *mu*)

To put this into real-world terms, the mean might represent something like average salary; Groups 1 and 2 might represent men and women. In that case, the hypothesis test above would suggest that the research predicts that men's salaries will be higher, on average, than those of women. The null hypothesis (a statement of no difference) would indicate that the salaries of men and women, on average, are equal.

You can test this hypothesis right away, since the data to do so are readily available. The **General Social Survey** (GSS) contains the variables needed to address this research question.

Of course, this format works for any variables that you choose. Presumably, if you are proposing a hypothesis, you should have an idea of how you will obtain observations (data) so that you can test that hypothesis. Otherwise, the research can go little further than speculation.

Inductive Research

This approach departs from what we think of as the traditional scientific method. With **inductive research**, we begin with the observations (data that have already been collected, or perhaps are collected first for the purpose of the research). Inductive research tends to be more descriptive and qualitative, though not exclusively so. Inductive research has a focus on studying observations for trends, patterns, or irregularities. With the discovery of such, theory and prior research are then consulted to help formulate your hypothesis.

BOX 1.1
THE GENERAL SOCIAL SURVEY

The National Opinion Research Center (NORC) at the University of Chicago administers the GSS. The GSS was started in 1972 and continues today. The data used for the examples in this book come from the latest available completed version of the GSS collected in 2016. According to NORC, with the exception of the U.S. Census, the GSS is the most frequently analyzed source of information in the social sciences. NORC acknowledges that there are at least 14,000 instances where the GSS has been used for articles in scholarly journals, books, and doctoral dissertations. Furthermore, it is estimated that more than 400,000 students annually use the GSS in their work.

The GSS contains many demographic and attitudinal questions, as well as rotating topics of special interest. A number of core questions have remained unchanged in each survey since 1972. This allows for rich longitudinal research about attitudes, opinions, and demographics in the United States. Topical questions appear sometimes for just one year; other times, they can appear for a period of years. Therefore, the GSS is versatile as a longitudinal data resource and a relevant cross-sectional resource.

To maximize the amount of information that can be collected in this massive interviewing project, the GSS uses a **split ballot design**, in which NORC's interviewers asked some questions in a random subsample of the households and asked other questions in other households. Some questions, including demographic items, were asked of all respondents. When we begin analyzing the GSS data, you will notice that some data items have a substantial number of respondents for whom data are marked as missing. For the most part, this refers to respondents who were not asked that particular question as a result of the split ballot design.

Although many items were asked of only a subsample of respondents, you can still take the responses as representative of the U.S. adult noninstitutionalized population, subject to normal sampling error. For more information about how the GSS data were collected, see Appendix B, Field Work and Interviewer Specifications, and Appendix C, General Coding Instructions, in the *General Social Survey 1972–2016 Cumulative Codebook* (Smith, Dalvern, Freese, & Hout, 2017).

Deductive Research

This approach directly involves what we think of as the scientific method. With **deductive research**, we begin with a theory and a hypothesis. So, at this point you will propose your hypothesis and at least one competing hypothesis (usually the statement of no difference described previously). Then we collect

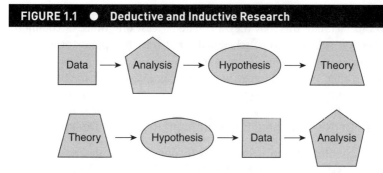

FIGURE 1.1 ● **Deductive and Inductive Research**

data (observations) to conduct the hypothesis test. Deductive research lends itself well to quantitative research. (See Figure 1.1 for a comparison of the two types of research.)

Research Designs

How to collect data (observations), as well as when and where to collect data, are critical concerns in developing an appropriate research design. You will need to consider available access to the population you wish to study, time, and other resources available. If you are studying a hard-to-reach or hard-to-identify population, that will be a pervasive foundation of your research, where you will need to address the difficulties and specify how you will overcome them. In proposing any research, it is important to be realistic about resources that are needed to carry out the research. Time, money, assistance, equipment, and other resources should be calculated and planned before embarking on the project. Without the resources needed to carry out the research, the project will fall short of an effective completion. With regard to time, you will need to determine the time period for data collection: Will the data be collected at one point in time, or will they be collected at more than one point in time to assess changes over the interval(s) of time?

Cross-Sectional Research Design

With **cross-sectional research**, the data are collected at one point in time. The data (observations) should represent a cross-section, or representative slice, of the population you intend to study. To obtain this cross-section, or representative sample, a variety of methods can be used (see Chapter 3).

Extra detail: To be clear, it's usually not possible to collect all data at the same second, or even in the same day, so that interval during which you collect data (say, 2 months) is considered as one point in time.

Longitudinal Research Design

If you decide to collect data from respondents at more than one point in time for the express purpose of comparison of change over time, then you would be conducting **longitudinal research**. There are a number of different ways to facilitate this, but they all share at least one thing in common: data collection will need to be scheduled for at least two points or intervals. If you are interested in multiple time points, such as collecting data annually for 10 years, then you would need to schedule and budget for the future data collection required in that design.

Repeated Cross-Sectional (Longitudinal) Research Design

This longitudinal design is exactly as it sounds: a repeated cross-section. In the **repeated cross-sectional research design**, a cross-section is taken at Time 1, then another independent cross-section of the same population is taken at Time 2. If the design calls for it, additional independent cross-sections can be taken at Time 3, Time 4, and so on, as many times as prescribed. Sampling methods used in each of the time periods should be the same or similar, unless you have documented evidence of improved sampling over time and you can demonstrate that the sample taken at each point in time is representative of the target population.

Fixed Sample Panel (Longitudinal) Research Design

The **fixed sample panel research design** starts just like a repeated cross-sectional design, with a cross-section at Time 1. However, any similarities with the former longitudinal design end there. At Time 2, the researcher must follow up with the same group selected for this original sample at Time 1. Also, it is important to point out that this is generally not something that can be effectively carried out spontaneously. In other words, it is not typical to begin a longitudinal research study not knowing whether you will use a repeated cross-sectional design or a fixed sample panel design. Part of the reason for this is that since the fixed sample panel design requires following up with the same respondents at a future point in time, the selection process is usually attuned to this so that you will have a better chance of having respondents follow up. Also, it is important to disclose to subjects that the nature of the study necessitates continuing data collection in the future and they will be contacted again. Moreover, there are strategies to increase retention of respondents over time, such as reminder e-mails, calls, postcards, thank-you notes, rewards for continued participation, and so on. It will be important to prepare a retention plan and budget up front at the very beginning of the research project.

This method has a tremendous advantage in that the change over time can be seen directly among the same respondents over time. The toll that must be paid for this advantage, however, can be high. Following up with the same respondents can be difficult, time-consuming, and costly. In some cases, the respondents may need to be located if they have changed addresses, stopped responding, gone away for vacation or other purposes, and so on. In other cases, respondents may not be able to be located at all. The two most obvious situations like this would be (a) a respondent's illness or death or (b) willful refusal of a respondent to cooperate with further data collection. Some of the retention methods described previously can be useful to improve continued response rates, but it is important to understand and to estimate what the attrition rate will be and how that will be handled. Will the sample diminish in size over time (in which case it will have to be larger than normal at the outset), or will there be a method of resampling for those cases that are lost? The latter can be useful for overall comparative analysis, but still does not address the loss of continuous subject data over time. (See Figure 1.2 for a comparison of the two types of research design.)

Cohort (Longitudinal) Research Design

The **cohort (longitudinal) research design** resembles the repeated cross-sectional design, but adds a requirement for the members who are to

FIGURE 1.2 ● Fixed Sample Panel Versus Repeated Cross-Section

Fixed Sample	Repeated Cross-Section
Pros	*Pros*
Follows same respondents Observe changes in individuals	Less expensive Easier to sample
Cons	*Cons*
Difficult to keep same respondents More expensive	Different respondents over time

BOX 1.2
MINI-CASE: FRAMINGHAM HEART STUDY

The Framingham Heart Study is a longitudinal study of the residents of Framingham, Massachusetts. The study began in 1948 and began a fixed sample panel design. Additional generations were later added to the study, but the design follows up with the same respondents over time to observe changes in outcome variables related to experiences of diet, exercise, and other factors. A great deal of knowledge about heart disease and the effects of cigarette smoking was first uncovered through this study. The research design enables the observation of particular behaviors to determine their role in health. For more information, go to the official website of the study: https://www .framinghamheartstudy.org.

be selected into the sample: They must have some common starting point. Typical cohorts include birth cohorts (born in the same year) and graduation cohorts (graduated from high school or college in the same year).

Terms

cohort (longitudinal) research design 7

cross-sectional research 5

deductive research 4

fixed sample panel research design 6

General Social Survey 3

inductive research 3

longitudinal research 6

repeated cross-sectional research design 6

split ballot design 4

Reference

Smith, T. W., Dalvern, M., Freese, J., & Hout, M. (2017). *General social surveys, 1972– 2016: Cumulative codebook*. Chicago, IL: National Opinion Research Center.

Variables and Measurement

Variables and Data

Variables and Hypotheses

An important part of scientific research is forming a **hypothesis**—a testable statement about the relationship between two or more variables. A **variable** is a logical grouping of attributes that can be observed and measured and is expected to vary from person to person in a population. In social science research, variables have two important properties—they are exhaustive and mutually exclusive.

First, in order for a variable to be **exhaustive**, there must be a comprehensive list of the attributes that make up the variable. In order to measure marital status, for example, one would need a complete list of marital statuses that make up the variable. If a researcher looking to measure individuals' marital satisfaction asked individuals to report their marital status as either married or not married, this would not be an exhaustive representation of the variable. In particular, limiting the measurement to only these two attributes does not effectively measure the marital status of individuals who are divorced, separated, widowed, or have never been married. Thus, an exhaustive variable provides a more comprehensive account of marital status categories. Second, in order to be **mutually exclusive**, an individual score can be in only one response category and no others. In the original example, if a separated individual marked both "married" and "not married," then the response is not mutually exclusive. When a score contains more than one attribute of a variable, then a survey respondent might be counted twice for a given attribute.

This problem is discussed in the context of frequencies and distributions in Chapter 4.

Independent and Dependent Variables

An important part of hypothesis development is identifying or speculating about *how* the relationship is hypothesized to exist between two variables—which is the independent variable and which is the dependent variable. Generally, we assume that the **independent variable (IV)** influences, or leads to some change in, the **dependent variable (DV)**.[1] Thinking of it another way, a change in the dependent variable is *dependent* upon the independent variable. As discussed in Chapter 1, the scientific rationale for this designation is largely rooted in theory and logic. However, even if a researcher does not have a clear idea of which is the independent and which is the dependent variable, even the most basic bivariate statistical procedures (e.g., tables and graphs) require that a designation between the two exists. For the sake of clarity, in addition to new and important terms being presented in **bold** font, this chapter uses a separate font to distinguish variables from other text.

Drawing on theory and data about individuals' life satisfaction (lifesatis) and their self-reported number of close friends (friends), one might hypothesize that life satisfaction *depends* upon the number of close friends one has. In other words, we are proposing that variations in friends—the independent variable—will lead to changes in life satisfaction (lifesatis)—the dependent variable.

Number of Close Friends (friends) (IV) → Life Satisfaction (lifesatis) (DV)

However, depending on the topic of investigation, the opposite designations could also be appropriate. Perhaps individuals who are satisfied with their lives are more likely to socialize and make friends. In this case, the hypothesis would suggest that lifesatis is the *independent* variable and friends is the *dependent* variable.

Life Satisfaction (lifesatis) (IV) → Number of Close Friends (friends) (DV)

Application to Statistics and Statistical Interpretation: Many commonly used statistical procedures—and most of those discussed later in this book—will be framed around which variable is the independent variable and which

---

[1] When you are reading through and interpreting statistical analyses in published research articles, you might come across other commonly used terms for these concepts. Here are some of the other names used to describe independent and dependent variables:

Dependent Variable: Outcome Variable, Response Variable, Criterion Variable
Independent Variable: Predictor Variable, Explanatory Variable, Experimental Variable, Stimulus

is the dependent variable. This designation is also important for interpreting bivariate tables (Chapter 4) and data visualizations (Chapter 5).

Directional Relationships

When presenting a hypothesis, researchers also identify which, if any, direction they expect the relationship to operate. Therefore, in addition to explaining *how* the relationship is expected to exist (i.e., which variable is independent versus dependent), a researcher should also identify the *type* of relationship as either positive, negative, or nondirectional.

A hypothesized **positive relationship** between variables is one where both variables are expected to operate in the same direction (either up or down) together. In the previous example, we might hypothesize that individuals with more close `friends` will report higher life satisfaction. This is an example of a hypothesized positive relationship—the hypothesis suggests that a higher number of close friendships (`friends`) will be associated with higher scores on self-reported life satisfaction (`lifesatis`). This is essentially the same as saying that lower numbers of close friendships will be related to lower scores on life satisfaction. Since both variables are expected to operate in the same direction, the hypothesized relationship is positive. In the simplest terms, one might even say, "I hypothesize a positive relationship between `friends` and `lifesatis`."

A hypothesized **negative relationship** between two variables is one where both variables are expected to operate *in opposite directions*—as one increases, the other decreases—and vice versa. Depending on theory and logic, a researcher might also propose that maintaining an extensive close social network could be overwhelming and intensely stressful compared to someone with a small, close-knit group of friends. In this case, more friends could lead to less satisfaction—a negative relationship. A higher number of close friendships (`friends`) will be associated with lower life satisfaction (`lifesatis`). Accordingly, a lower number of close friendships will lead to higher life satisfaction.

Some hypotheses are **nondirectional**. If the study is exploratory and there is no reason to hypothesize a directional relationship, then the hypothesized relationship is left open. A researcher might hypothesize that there is a relationship between the size of someone's `social network` and the `number of dates` he or she goes on each week. However, she might choose to leave this hypothesis *nondirectional* if she is unsure of the direction of the relationship. For instance, those with many friends might be too busy in their social lives to go on many dates. On the other hand, those with a large social circle might have more opportunities to go on frequent dates with new people.

Some types of variables are not suited for directional hypotheses. The relationship between marital status (`marstat`) and number of close friends (`friends`) would be an example of this. Try and imagine the hypothesized direction between these two variables. It would be impossible because `marital` status does not operate on a continuum—it does not increase or decrease. In other words, it has a different *measurement*. This is one reason why understanding how variables are measured, or their "level of measurement," is an extremely important element in hypothesis development, research design, data analysis, and the interpretation of results.

Levels of Variable Measurement

One way of looking at the way variables are measured is based on the characteristics of the variables—whether, and how, they operate on a continuum. There are two primary levels of measurement for variables (with other subcategories within them based on additional criteria): categorical and quantitative.[2] These levels of measurement are key to guiding all statistical analyses because some types of variables have attributes that others do not.

Categorical Variables

Categorical variables are based on a series of categories that do not have meaningful numbers associated with them. There are several types of categorical variables, each discussed below: nominal variables, dichotomous variables, and ordinal variables.

Nominal Variables

Nominal variables are simply a list of different categories that cannot be rank ordered in any way. They are used to describe membership in mutually exclusive categories, but aside from assignment into a particular group, nominal variables have no other properties. Marital status (never married, married, divorced, separated, widowed) is an example of a commonly used nominal variable—individuals can be in one marital status category or another and nothing else is known about the categories. As the lowest level of measurement, nominal variables have the least amount of information; therefore, analysis and interpretation with nominal variables are limited to the most basic statistical analyses.

Given that quantitative social science data are coded numerically, the nominal variables are usually represented by arbitrary numbers (i.e., the number 1 could just as easily represent "never married" as the number 34 or 83 or 5). The number is simply a numerical identification code for that characteristic. The

---

[2] In your research, you might come across other terms that are used to identify the different levels of variable measurement:

Nominal: Categorical, String
Ordinal: Rank Order
Quantitative: Interval/Ratio, Continuous, Equal-Interval

meaning of those numbers is recorded in a **codebook**, a document that provides details on numerical codes and measurement to help researchers conduct and interpret their statistical analyses. For an example of a codebook entry, see Figure 2.1.

Dichotomous Variables

Dichotomous variables are those that have only two responses. While these variables might technically be considered nominal (since one either places in the category or not), they are often considered a special case since their binary nature is an attribute that other measures do not have. Among the most commonly used dichotomous variables in the social sciences is sex (male or female). Other examples of dichotomous variables are measurements that yield yes/no or true/false responses. As later chapters will show, there are special statistical procedures that can be used to conduct analysis using dichotomous variables.

Ordinal Variables

Ordinal variables are categories that specify a specific characteristic of an individual or individuals *but can be rank ordered*, thereby giving information about an individual's placement relative to others on the scale. These variables have an added property of rank-ordered attributes from lowest to highest—these numbers are usually classified in quantitative data as sequential numbers. For

---

FIGURE 2.1 ● Example of a Codebook Entry

FIGURE 2.1 identifies different parts of a codebook entry used to keep details about variables, their codes, and other characteristics.

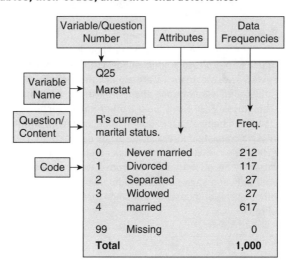

example, self-reported life satisfaction (lifesatis) is measured with an ordinal level of measurement if individuals are categorized as (1) very dissatisfied through (7) very satisfied. Because there is a logical order to the categories, we know that individuals who are *very satisfied* are more satisfied than those who report being *very unsatisfied*. However, an ordered scale is still limited in the information it provides because we have no information on just *how much more* satisfied they are—that information is only present in quantitative variables.

Quantitative (Interval/Ratio) Variables

Quantitative variables are the highest level of measurement. These variables have meaningful numbers associated with them that refer to specific quantities. For example, one's actual age is a quantitative variable because the numbers are quantitatively meaningful (e.g., 21, 17, 91). Unlike ordinal variables, such as social class, quantitative variables allow us to know *exactly how different* individuals are relative to others. We know that someone who is 21 years old is 4 years older than someone who is 17—because the spacing of the intervals is equal. Therefore, quantitative variables give us the most information. For additional clarification on levels of variable measurement, see Box 2.1. One way to differentiate a quantitative variable from other variable types is to ask, "Would I be able to plot the variable's characteristics like coordinates on a graph?" If the answer is no, then it is not a quantitative variable (see Figure 2.2).

BOX 2.1
LEVELS OF VARIABLE MEASUREMENT AND PLAYING CARDS

A useful analogy for the difference between nominal, ordinal, and quantitative variables can be found in a standard 52-card deck of playing cards. First, in many card games, *the suits* (diamond, spade, club, and heart) are not rank ordered in any way. These categories are similar to nominal variables since they have no underlying assumptions about ordering or sequence—they are just different categories. *Face cards*, on the other hand, can be logically rank ordered from lowest to highest (Jack, Queen, King, and Ace). With face cards, however, there is no consistent interval that exists between them—just a logical rank ordering. The remainder of the deck can be thought of as discrete quantitative variables because they range from 2 to 10, with equal intervals assumed to exist between each number. Additionally, the card colors represent a dichotomous level of measurement since there are only two possibilities: black and red.

FIGURE 2.2 ● Nominal, Ordinal, and Interval/Ratio Data

FIGURE 2.2 helps illustrate the difference between nominal, ordinal, and interval/ratio data. Using a Cartesian plane, it would be impossible to meaningfully plot coordinates for `city of birth`, a nominal variable, and `social class`, an ordinal variable (Panel A). On the other hand, one *can* plot coordinates for `age` and `height` because both are interval/ratio variables (Panel B).

Panel A: City of Birth and Social Class

City of Birth

Panel B: Age and Height

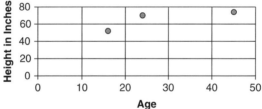

Age

The Zero-Point

An **interval variable** is a quantitative variable with a zero-point that is arbitrary. In other words, a zero does not necessarily imply the absence of the construct. On the other hand, a **ratio variable** has a meaningful zero, whereby a zero indicates that there is a complete absence of that variable. For the purposes of the statistical procedures and interpretations discussed in this book, the difference between interval and ratio variables is less important than their quantitative nature; therefore, these variables will be referred to as either quantitative or interval/ratio variables.

Continuous and Discrete Quantitative Variables

There are some additional properties of variables that researchers sometimes take into consideration when designing a study and analyzing data. One such property is based on the proportions that exist between values. A **continuous quantitative variable** has an infinite number of possible values between two units. Using `weight` as an example, the interval between 179 and 180 pounds is theoretically infinite, as the decimals can extend infinitely beyond 179.7898. On the other hand, a **discrete quantitative variable** can take on only fixed values that are positive integers. For example, `number of close friends` is a discrete quantitative variable—the value cannot be infinitely reduced and can only be represented by whole numbers.

Transforming Variable Types

There is a hierarchy across the different variable types based on the amount of information they provide about a concept (e.g., interval/ratio variables have more information than ordinal variables, which have more information than nominal variables). Often, researchers are interested in transforming a variable into one with different properties. Quantitative variables can be **transformed** into categorical variables—that is, we can take the information from a quantitative variable and make it into a variable with the characteristics of those variables with less information. However, we cannot take information from a categorical variable and make it quantitative. For example, knowing someone's exact `height` would allow a researcher to classify him or her as short, average, or tall (an ordinal scale), but knowing if someone is short, average, or tall would not allow a researcher to extrapolate the person's actual `height`.

There are two commonly accepted exceptions to this rule. The first is **Likert-type items**, where an individual chooses from a range of possible responses that reflect his or her feelings, knowledge, or attitudes. For example, a common Likert-type item ranges from (1) *strongly disagree* to (7) *strongly agree*. These items are sometimes treated as quantitative variables in statistical analyses and interpretation. As such, researchers assume that the single-unit difference between a (1) and a (2) ranking is roughly the same as the single-unit difference between a (4) and a (5) ranking. Another exception to the transformation is the use of midpoints to identify a specific numerical amount when only a range is known. For example, a variable that asks for individuals' `annual income` with ranges (e.g., $50,000–$60,000) can be transformed into a quantitative variable by taking the midpoint of each range to transform the ordinal range into a meaningful quantity (e.g., $55,000).

Application to Statistics and Statistical Interpretation: Later chapters demonstrate the importance of levels of measurement of dependent and independent variables for statistical analysis and interpretation. For now, it is important to take note that levels of variable measurement are among the most important aspects of research design and largely depend on the way the data collection instrument is constructed.

Types of Relationships

Causal Relationships

One important consideration when developing a hypothesis is whether or not research is testing for a **causal relationship**, one where the independent variable *causes* a change in the dependent variable. In order to confirm that a causal relationship exists, researchers must establish three criteria. The criteria are discussed using the following information:

Hypothesis: Individuals with more close friends are more satisfied with their lives.

Independent Variable: Number of Close Friends (friends)

Dependent Variable: Life Satisfaction (lifesatis)

Direction: Positive

First, the variables must be **correlated**, meaning they operate together in some way—they are associated. If we see that friends and lifesatis both change in some way in relation to the other, then we know that the variables are correlated in some way.

"Friends and lifesatis are related—when one changes, so does the other one."

Second, **temporal precedence** must be established for the independent variable; that is, the independent variable (cause) must occur *before* the dependent variable (effect) in time. Thus, an increase in close friendships must precede an increase in life satisfaction (X → Y).

"Friends increases *and then* lifesatis increases."

Third, and usually the most difficult criterion to establish, is that there should be no intervening factor that influences both variables. In this case, income might influence both variables, making it appear as though there is a causal relationship between friends and lifesatis where there is none (see Figure 2.3).

FIGURE 2.3   ●   Causal Relationships

FIGURE 2.3 illustrates how income might be independently associated with both friends *and* happiness, making a relationship between the two *appear* causal.

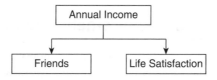

"Individuals with higher incomes (income) have more close friends (friends)." "Individuals with higher incomes (income) have higher life satisfaction (lifesatis)."

Therefore, it might appear as though close friendships *cause* greater life satisfaction—but the relationship operates through income.

As discussed in Chapter 1, there are many different techniques to try to limit the effect of these intervening variables. In survey-based studies, researchers use longitudinal research designs in order to measure variables at two or more points in time. In such a study, researchers might explore changes in the size of friendship networks and life satisfaction over time.

When trying to establish a cause–effect relationship, experimental research is commonly considered the scientific gold standard. Under the proper experimental conditions—which includes randomization into control and experimental groups—intervening variables can be "controlled." Because selection into the experimental and control group was randomized, the control group is assumed to be like the experimental group in all other ways. Given that assumption, researchers can be more confident that they have eliminated the possibility of intervening factors, like income in the previous example.

Correlational Relationships

Some researchers are less interested in establishing a cause-and-effect relationship than simply exploring whether, how, and how strongly two variables are related. These are known as **correlational studies**, the most common of which is survey research. The primary goal of correlational research is to show whether a change in one variable is associated with change in another variable—and possibly identify the direction of the relationship.

Application to Statistics and Statistical Interpretation: Understanding whether or not the relationship between two variables is causal or correlational is important in order for researchers to avoid drawing erroneous or misleading conclusions by making causal statements when the relationship is not, in fact, a causal one. For example, if a survey research team were to interpret the results of its analysis and conclude, "Friends make you more satisfied with life," the findings would be misleading. If these researchers did not properly account (or "control") for other differences between individuals that can affect friendship and life satisfaction, such as income, then the relationship is only correlational, not causal.

Research Design and Measurement Quality

When dealing with variables, whether dependent or independent, measurement quality is an important element in the research process. Since social, behavioral, and health scientists often deal with concepts that are difficult to define and measure, there are several approaches to substantiate variables to improve their value for the research community.

Operationalization and Conceptualization

When researchers are testing hypotheses about dependent and independent variables, they must provide precise definitions of their main concepts and their measurement. Operationalization and conceptualization are the processes whereby researchers define and list the methods of observation for specific variables and measurements.

Conceptualization refers to the meaning, or conceptual definition, of a specific construct that a researcher proposes for her study. By providing a conceptual definition, the researcher is allowing readers to know exactly what she means when using that term. For example, if a study is examining whether moving leads to increases in children's behavior problems, one must first clearly define what is meant by "moving." Indeed, the term *moving* could mean any number of things from fine motor skills all the way to international migration. In order to conceptualize "moving," a researcher must provide a precise definition of what the term implies. In this case, moving means "a permanent relocation from one residence to another for longer than 1 year."

Conceptualization is the process of defining the concepts under study to clarify their meaning for the purposes of the research—and those meanings might differ from the conceptualization another researcher provides in another study. It would be confusing and counterproductive to conduct a study where no statement was made about what was meant by the terms being used. Perhaps others would recognize and understand moving to mean something completely different.

Operationalization is describing how the researcher empirically measures, or observes, the construct. While conceptualization entails providing a precise definition of a concept, the next step is to identify indicators of the measure. This process establishes the criteria being used to determine whether something exists versus when it does not. For example, a researcher might conceptualize a close friend as "a platonic associate who provides emotional support, instrumental support, or companionship." Operationalization is the process whereby a researcher describes the operations involved in observing or measuring the concept. Here, a researcher must describe *how* he will empirically observe whether a close friendship exists or not. Identifying a number of indicators, like those in Figure 2.4, would be one way to operationalize close friendship. In addition to the indicators in the figure, consider the multitude of alternate ways a researcher might operationalize close friendship.

Internal and External Validity

Researchers are always concerned about the legitimacy of their research design and results. As such, scientific research emphasizes the importance of

FIGURE 2.4 ● Conceptualizing and Operationalizing Close Friendship

FIGURE 2.4 presents one way of defining (i.e., conceptualizing) and making determinations about (i.e., operationalizing) close friendship. The following details are based on research on close friendships over the life cycle (Gillespie, Frederick, Harari, & Grov, 2015; Gillespie, Lever, Frederick, & Royce, 2015).

WHAT IS A CLOSE FRIEND?

A nonfamily platonic relationship where individuals provide emotional support, instrumental support, and companionship.

MEASURING CLOSE FRIENDSHIP

Expressive Support: You can talk with this person about intimate topics (i.e., sex life).
Instrumental Support: You can call on this person to help you if you are in trouble late at night.
Companionship: You expect this person to do something with you to celebrate your birthday.

internal and external validity. **Internal validity** is the degree to which a researcher can demonstrate that a causal relationship exists between variables. **External validity** refers to the applicability of a study to a wider, or more generalized, audience. Each of these concepts is discussed below, with some cautionary threats for each type.

Internal Validity

Internal validity is a concept used widely within experimental research to assert the legitimacy of a causal relationship between a dependent and an independent variable. As discussed above, researchers are often concerned with saying X *causes* Y; however, issues with the experiment can compromise researchers' ability to make such a causal statement. The following section highlights eight common problems that can occur in experiments that influence causal results. While some of these problems might seem unavoidable, researchers should try to reduce problems whenever possible.

What if a participant in an experiment knows the answers to posttest questions because he or she was asked the same questions in the pretest? This is known as a **testing effect.** For example, a statistics professor is interested in assessing how effective her teaching methods are by using a variation on the classical experimental design. She gives students a questionnaire (pretest) about their math aptitude at the beginning of the semester, teaches a semester-long course on statistics, and then gives the same exact test at the end of the semester (posttest). There is a possibility that students' responses on the posttest are higher not because of the professor's effective teaching methods, but because students remembered the questions, had time to think them over, or paid closer attention to areas they identified as difficult. In this case, the professor's teaching (independent variable/stimulus) would appear to be effective since the students' math aptitude scores were higher—but some of the difference could be related to the pretest matching the posttest.

What if I change the pretest and posttest to avoid this testing effect? If the same professor chooses to use a different posttest measurement at the end of the semester, not the same test as the pretest, there is a possibility of **instrumentation bias.** It is possible that the questions on the first test were easier, harder, or perceived as easier or harder than the earlier questions. In this sense, it would appear that students scored differently on math aptitude not because of the information presented in the course, but because of changes in the level of difficulty in the pretest and posttest instruments.

What if something important happens before the test is over? A research professor at Market University is interested in exploring how participation in university groups influences the size of students' social networks. He hypothesizes that the more students participate in university clubs, the larger their social network will be (i.e., a positive relationship where the independent variable is participating in clubs and the dependent variable is size of social network). Students in the experimental group must sign up for three social clubs on campus—the control group is advised to avoid joining groups for the duration of the experiment. However, if a flu outbreak influences the way students interact with one another, this epidemic could influence the outcome. This **history effect** influences the results of the experiment because a large-scale event (flu outbreak), not the stimulus (participation in clubs), influenced the outcome (social network size).

What if the people in the experimental and control groups are different from each other? This would be an example of **selectivity.** In the previous example, if the most gregarious students in the class are in the experimental group and those in the control group are the shyer and more reserved students, it might seem that there is a relationship between group affiliations and social network size. However, the relationship might be merely a reflection of this limitation in the experimental design. In research, this is known as

selection bias. This can happen when the experimental and control groups differ along some important characteristic related to the study.

What happens when people mature between the time the experiment begins and the time it ends? This is known as the **maturation effect.** Individuals might respond differently to a pretest than they otherwise would had time not passed. For example, individuals in the group affiliation and social networks experiment might have more friends at the end of the experiment simply because they have matured—perhaps over the course of the semester they developed different opinions on the importance of friendships and participation in university clubs. Again, this threat to internal validity creates the appearance of a causal relationship when one might not be present.

What happens when people leave the experiment? Experimental mortality occurs when people leave the experiment. Individuals can leave an experiment for a number of reasons (e.g., death, boredom, or moral disagreement with the subject matter). At best, this can limit the sample size; at worst, it can lead to selection bias. For example, if students in the experimental group to study the effects of group affiliation chose to leave because they are anxious about making new friends, then the experimental group might tend toward those more gregarious people who make friends easily.

What happens when the experimenter is biased because he or she knows who is in the experimental and who is in the control group? Experimenter bias occurs when the person running the experiment already knows who is in the experimental and control groups and then, perhaps unconsciously, treats them differently. In this case, the experimenter influences the interactions and feelings of the individuals in one group more so than the other. Researchers have developed a way to deal with the potential of this—they do what is called a **double-blind experiment,** which means that the experimenter does not know who is in the experimental or control groups.

What happens when people score very low or very high on the pretest? If the results vary because pretest scores were in the extreme regions, this might reflect **statistical regression toward the mean.** When individuals have very low scores at the pretest, there is a tendency to tend toward an average in the posttest. For example, students who score far below average on a pretest for math aptitude will tend to move closer toward the mean on the posttest. This makes it appear as though those students performed better because of the professor's teaching effectiveness, but they did so because students who scored in the lower extreme trended upward on the posttest. This threat to validity is based on the reliability of the instrument, or the ability to yield the same results with the same instrument after repeated measurement (discussed later).

Each of these threats to internal validity influences the way an experimenter draws conclusions about causal relationships—perhaps making it appear that the independent variable causes a change in the dependent variable when it does not. One way to improve internal validity is to create sound arguments and use caution when developing a rigorous research design. Another type of validity, external validity, points to whether the results of a given study are applicable to other groups and contexts.

External Validity

More often than not, social science researchers are interested in conducting studies and applying the results to larger groups. External validity is the extent to which the results of a study are applicable to other contexts. For example, a researcher who surveys his course to explore how `sleep habits` influence `school performance` would have low generalizability (external validity) since the sample consists only of college students. Therefore, the study's results might not apply to students at other grade levels—indeed, they might not even apply to students at other universities. Two ways to improve external validity is to (a) employ appropriate sampling procedures and (b) replicate the study on other groups to confirm the results. Additionally, researchers should aim to achieve high response rates and low dropout rates, which can help avoid a biased sample population.

Measurement Validity and Reliability

The previous section outlined two types of validity as they relate to the design of a study—whether researchers can confidently establish a causal relationship (internal validity) and whether the results apply to a wider group (external validity). However, in addition to the overall study design, researchers are also concerned with the quality of the measurements used to measure specific concepts. Measurement validity and reliability are ways that researchers inspect the quality of a measurement. Each, in its own respect, helps researchers assess whether their measurements are sound ones. However, keep in mind that these are not all-or-nothing assessments of a measurement. Instead, validity and reliability operate on a continuum from low to high—and researchers should strive to have both high validity and high reliability.

Measurement Validity

Measurement validity is an assessment of the quality of a measure to accurately tap into a target concept. There are four types of validity commonly encountered by researchers looking to assess the quality of their measures: face validity, content validity, criterion-based validity, and construct validity.

Does the measurement seem to be an accurate measurement of the concept? When a measurement seems to intuitively measure a target construct, the measure is presumed to have **face validity.** Face validity is a superficial assessment of whether or not the measurement "looks good at face value." Under some circumstances, low face validity might increase the overall measurement validity by helping avoid interviewer bias and social desirability.

Are all components of the construct being measured? If so, then the measurement has **content validity.** In order to be high in content validity, a measurement must assess the concept under study in a comprehensive way. This is especially important when measuring complex or nebulous concepts, such as well-being, where multiple dimensions are explored (e.g., physical wellness, emotional stability, life satisfaction) in order to form a measurement that comprehensively represents the entire construct.

Does the measurement correlate with other measures or outcomes? If so, it is thought to be high in **criterion-based validity.** Criterion-based validity is based on holding the measure against other criteria. When a measurement is determined to correlate with other theoretically relevant measures in the study, it has **concurrent validity.** If the measure corresponds to some theoretically relevant pre-established criterion (e.g., GRE scores and graduate school performance), then it has established **predictive validity.**

Is the instrument truly measuring the construct under study and not some other construct? If the measurement is an adequate assessment of the construct, then it is thought to have **construct validity.** For example, if researchers use an instrument to measure self-esteem in adolescence, they would need to confirm that their measure was tapping into self-esteem and not some other (possibly related) concept, such as depression, anxiety, or loneliness.

Researchers must be transparent by (a) demonstrating the effectiveness of a given measure and (b) identifying limitations and discussing the ways such limitations could influence the results.

Reliability

In addition to being accurate, measurements must also be consistent (i.e., have **reliability**). When a measure produces consistent results after repeated administration, it is reliable. For example, in survey research, if an open-ended response option is used to measure the number of dates a college student went on in a year's time, the answer could yield less reliable results given that a precise answer might not be known and a respondent might guess (which means it is not a very reliable measure). On the other hand, a set of ranges might help an individual provide an approximate response, leading to more consistency in the results. There are several ways to help ensure a measure is reliable. First, make sure questions are written clearly. Also, make sure closed-ended questions have a realistic number of response options from which to choose, and possibly an option for "don't know/NA."

Testing for Reliability

This section discusses several tests to assess the reliability of a measurement. First, **test–retest reliability** estimates a measurement's reliability based on the consistency of results after repeated administration. Responses from measures taken at Time 1 and Time 2 are assessed to estimate the stability of the measure over the two time points. A reliable question should elicit a similar response from one administration to the next. Second, **alternate forms reliability** refers to consistency between two different versions of a measure that probes the same construct. Third, **split-test reliability** groups similar items in a measurement instrument into two sets of equivalent items that are split into two halves. The scores from each half are compared to determine the degree of correlation between them. Correlation should be high among questions reliably measuring the same concept. Last, **Cronbach's alpha** is a statistical summary measure of the **internal consistency** of data collected across multiple items that form a scale. While there are no hard and fast rules regarding interpretation of Cronbach's alpha, the higher the value of Cronbach's alpha, the more consistent the items. For example, a Cronbach's alpha of .83 indicates that 83% of the variation is shared across the items.

Conclusion

In order to test a bivariate or multivariate hypothesis, one needs to define variables as either independent or dependent. If applicable, the direction of the hypothesis should also be stated, keeping in mind that certain types of variables (e.g., nominal) are not designed for directional relationships. Once a clear and testable hypothesis is developed, a research design must be chosen, keeping in mind both internal and external validity. Importantly, avoid hypothesizing a causal relationship if the research design is ill equipped to establish such relationships. After the research design has been chosen, a researcher must develop accurate and consistent measurements for the concepts under study. Each of these guidelines helps researchers target and address issues of precision that quality research must take into consideration. In order to fully grasp the concepts in the chapters to follow, an understanding of these concepts is necessary.

Terms

alternate forms reliability 25

categorical variables 12

causal relationship 17

codebook 13

conceptualization 19

concurrent validity 24

construct validity 24

content validity 24

continuous quantitative
variable 16

correlated 17

correlational studies 18

criterion-based validity 24

Cronbach's alpha 25

dependent variable (DV) 10

dichotomous variables 13

discrete quantitative variable 16

double-blind experiment 22

exhaustive 9

experimental mortality 22

experimenter bias 22

external validity 20

face validity 24

history effect 21

hypothesis 9

independent variable (IV) 10

instrumentation bias 21

internal consistency 25

internal validity 20

interval variable 15

Likert-type items 16

maturation effect 22

measurement validity 23

mutually exclusive 9

negative relationship 11

nominal variables 12

nondirectional 11

operationalization 19

ordinal variables 13

positive relationship 11

predictive validity 24

quantitative variables 14

ratio variable 15

reliability 25

selection bias 22

selectivity 21

split-test reliability 25

statistical regression toward
the mean 22

temporal precedence 17

testing effect 20

test–retest reliability 25

transformed 16

variable 9

References

Gillespie, B. J., Frederick, D., Harari, L., & Grov, C. (2015). Homophily, close friendship, and life satisfaction among gay, lesbian, heterosexual, and bisexual men and women. *PLoS One, 10*(6), e0128900.

Gillespie, B. J., Lever, J., Frederick, D., & Royce, T. (2015). Close adult friendships, gender, and the life cycle. *Journal of Social and Personal Relationships, 32*(6), 709–736.

How to Sample and Collect Data for Analysis

Why Use a Sample?

Typically, the **intended (target) population** is too large to permit data collection from each member. Unless the intended population is very small and accessible, time and money are the first barriers that would prevent data collection from all members of the population.

Data collection from each subject would constitute a **census**. The U.S. Census is probably the one with which you are most familiar. It was initiated in 1790 and, by order of the U.S. Constitution, is conducted every 10 years. Since a census is generally not feasible in scientific research, a representative subset (a sample) offers the opportunity to learn about the population in a manner that is feasible. Without a high-quality sample, it simply is not possible to answer research questions with any certainty.

Probability Sampling Methods

When the probability of any member of the intended (target) population to be selected into the sample is known in advance, we say that this is a **probability sample**. It is important to note that the probabilities of all the members of the intended (target) population do not have to all be the same, but they must be calculable. We often refer to these various probability samples as random samples. Random samples are selected by chance alone.

Simple Random Sample

By selecting each case solely on the basis of chance, where all cases have an equal chance of being selected into the sample, this creates a **simple random sample**.

Photo by Billy Wagner.

PHOTO 3.1 Random selection by lots of dice

You can roll dice, flip a coin, pick numbers out of a hat, or use some other purely chance-driven method to select cases. You cannot, however, just look at a list and choose "randomly" yourself. As much as it seems like people's behavior is random, the human brain is not capable of random behavior.

Systematic Random Sample

Systematic random sampling is a method of sampling where every Nth member in the total population is chosen for inclusion in the sample after the first member of the sample is selected at random from among the first N members of the population. N is the ratio computed by dividing the population size by the intended sample size.

Systematic Random Sampling: Periodicity

Periodicity occurs when the sequence of respondents or other elements (list, physical structure) varies in a regular pattern. If there is a regular pattern among the list of elements and the value of N used in systematic random sampling causes some types of elements to be selected more than others, this creates a situation where, indeed, the sample is not random at all.

For example, suppose you needed to sample students in a classroom and the classroom contains 20 students in five rows of four students (from the front to the back of the room). Your desired sample size is five. By computing the ratio 20/5, the result is *k*, 4. So you choose the first student at random from the first four, then each fourth student. Then you would end up with students all in the same row. They may be all students in a particular row: the front row, the back row, or some other row. This is problematic if you intend to suggest that the sample is truly random. Among other things, it has been our experience that students in the first row of a large class tend to have different characteristics than the total student population in that class, as the sample would emerge if the first random selection between 1 and 4 was 1, illustrated in Figure 3.1.

Another situation that might present an obvious problem is one involving a study about gardening. Suppose periodicity leads to all houses on the southwest corner of the block being sampled. Since this is a study about gardening, the role of sunlight probably has an effect, so there is a real, direct effect on the study. Even without knowledge of a direct effect, a regular pattern in a so-called random sample is enough to bring the sampling into question. So, it is important to watch for periodicity if using any kind of systematic random sampling.

Stratified Random Sample

Stratified random sampling is a method of sampling achieved by dividing the population into subgroups based on one or more variables that are related to the research question, then drawing a simple random (or perhaps systematic random) sample from each of the designated subgroups.

A sample can be stratified using a single variable. Multiple variables can also be used simultaneously to give a more precise representative framework to the sample. Ultimately, which variables are used to stratify will depend on your

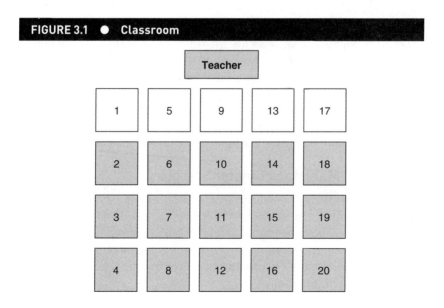

FIGURE 3.1 ● Classroom

specific research question, as well as the weaknesses in the research design due to the difficulties in identifying and/or finding members of the population.

Proportionate Stratified Random Sample

With **proportionate stratified sampling**, the size of the sample drawn from each subgroup is proportional to the size of that particular subgroup in the population. With this method, your sample is guaranteed to look like the population in terms of the categories of the variable or variables by which you have elected to stratify the sample.

This method is useful when you want to be sure that the sample truly resembles a smaller replica of the population with regard to the one or more variables by which you divide the population. For example, if you want to make sure that the sample is truly proportional to the population with regard to gender and/or race/ethnicity, proportionate stratified sampling is a good option.

Disproportionate Stratified Random Sample

With **disproportionate stratified sampling**, the size of the sample drawn from each subgroup is disproportional to the size of that subgroup in the population.

This method is useful if you are comparing subgroups of the population and one or more of those subgroups is particularly small. For instance, if you are taking a sample from a population that is overwhelmingly female, but you are interested in studying the comparative experiences of females and males or those who are cisgender and transgender, it will be necessary to ensure that you have a large enough sample size to be able to make a meaningful comparison between the two groups under investigation.

Suppose your research question calls for a comparison between females and males. If the population (say, students in a particular major at a particular university campus) is made up of 90% females and 10% males, your sample size would either need to be significantly large to ensure enough males would be selected to generalize on the experience of males at this particular university, or you could stratify your small sample. If your sample size is set at 30 (because of budget, time, etc.), you can select 15 females and 15 males, rather than ending up with only 3 males (or possibly fewer, due to the distribution of random sampling).

Cluster and Multistage Cluster Samples

Cluster sampling is a useful strategy when a sampling frame (a complete list of respondents) is not available. This is often the case for large populations spread out across a wide geographic area or for large populations spread among many different organizations. In these cases, it is highly unlikely that these populations would have a master list, but there may be lists among smaller clusters, such as organizations.

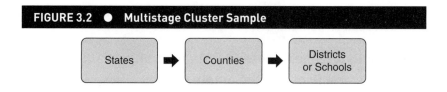

FIGURE 3.2 ● Multistage Cluster Sample

States ➡ Counties ➡ Districts or Schools

What if you wanted to take a random sample of all the fifth-graders in the United States? Would you be surprised to learn that there is no list of all the fifth graders in the United States? If there were a list, where would it be, or who would have it? President Trump does not have such a list, nor did President Obama. There is not a complete list at the U.S. Department of Education, either. Who is keeping track of our nation's fifth-graders?

It turns out that the local school districts and schools themselves are the best and most reliable places to find those lists of fifth-graders (and presumably students in other grades, too). So, you could start by sampling a set of large clusters: U.S. states. Then, for the next step, you could sample smaller clusters: counties within each of the states already selected. Then, finally, you can move on to districts or schools (there are lists of school districts and schools for each county) and randomly select schools from the list. Some counties are larger than others with regard to population and therefore schools and students. Some counties will have multiple districts; others will not. You may need to do an extra sampling of districts in the counties with larger populations, even though this step will not be necessary in the counties with much smaller populations. Since we know that there is a known list of counties in each state, of districts and schools within each of those states, and of students within each school, we know that we can get a random sample obtained by randomly selecting choices at each stage of the cluster sample. Not only will this allow you to maintain the rigor of a random sample, but in many cases, it may also save precious resources. If this data collection requires a physical presence, by first narrowing the frame to clusters at the state level, you have minimized travel expenses and time by limiting the sample to, say, seven states, instead of 50 plus the District of Columbia.

Nonprobability Sampling Methods

When the probability of members of the intended (target) population being selected into the sample is not known, we say this is a **nonprobability sample**. Probability samples are better than nonprobability samples, ceteris paribus (all else being equal), since probability samples that are drawn properly can offer a guarantee of representativeness. Of course, it is of paramount importance that the sample be representative of the intended population; otherwise, whether the sample is of the probability or nonprobability variety will not save it from being an ineffective tool to analyze the population. As discussed next, there are ways to obtain representative nonprobability samples and validate the success of that representativeness.

Why Would Anyone Choose to Obtain a Nonprobability Sample Over a Probability Sample?

Sometimes, a probability sample is not feasible or even possible at all. If you wish to sample a hard-to-identify or hard-to-reach population, probability sampling may not work. Therefore, nonprobability sampling emerges as the option. Just as with probability sampling, nonprobability sampling can be done in different ways. Some of these methods, executed properly, can go a long way toward providing a representative and valid sample. Others may not be of much use, depending on how much generalizability is required in your research design.

Convenience

One type of nonprobability sampling, **convenience sampling**, is exactly as it appears: It is done entirely at the convenience of the researcher. As you might imagine, this type of sampling is the least useful since it is neither systematic nor random. Therefore, this method will not produce a representative sample and will offer little to no ability to generalize results from the sample to a larger population. It is also known as availability sampling or haphazard sampling. So, why bother? In extreme cases where there is no other option, convenience sampling is a place to start; this might lead to further contacts and allow for some better structured sampling at a later point in time. It might also afford a researcher a faster opportunity to explore some themes early in the research that might be used to help develop a sampling frame for the main research question(s).

Snowball

Another method of nonprobability sampling, **snowball sampling**, is useful for sampling hard-to-reach populations. Neither freezing temperatures nor snow are required; this sampling can be done in the heat if necessary. Snowball sampling is sometimes also called chain sampling or chain referral.

The essential component of snowball sampling is that respondents refer the researcher to other respondents who meet the parameters of the target/intended population. Those referred respondents refer others, and so on. So, it is important that at least some members of the target population know each other; otherwise, respondents would not have the knowledge of whom to refer. Depending on the population, this method may be particularly helpful for researching populations that are geographically distributed (Heckathorn, 2011).

The initial respondents, those selected before any referrals are made, are still chosen using a convenience or availability approach. If each respondent refers more than one new person who participated, each successive level of referrals will generate a larger number of respondents, as shown in Figure 3.3. Here, you

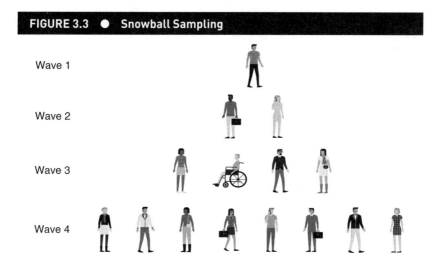

FIGURE 3.3 ● Snowball Sampling

Wave 1

Wave 2

Wave 3

Wave 4

can see the sampling mechanism working like a snowball rolling down a slope gaining mass geometrically (or at least that's how it looks in cartoons!). In any case, the successive levels of referrals continue until the desired sample size is reached.

Respondent-Driven Sampling

Respondent-driven sampling (RDS) is a sophisticated improvement on snowball sampling. If done properly, this method affords the researchers using it greater ability to generalize than does standard snowball sampling. RDS uses incentives to improve the representativeness of the sample. Incentives go to the respondent who refers other potential respondents. This initial respondent gets an incentive for each subject who is successfully recruited into the study (reducing bias and increasing potential new subjects since the original subject will be rewarded). A secondary incentive is also given to future subjects if they are successfully recruited into the study (further reducing bias).

Why are incentives necessary? Without incentives, respondent self-selection is a bigger problem: Those who participate may have some characteristic that leads them to participate while others may not, so the sample would be biased along the lines of that characteristic. For example, perhaps only nonworking members of a population respond, while those employed full-time do not—presumably because of time constraints. The sample we would get would be biased and neither representative of the population nor particularly generalizable. It is important to keep track of respondent referrals and prevent those respondents who refer other potential respondents who might be professionals from referring too many respondents. The temptation may exist depending on the nature of the incentive. Too many referrals from just one person begins to approach standard snowball sampling and could diminish the positive aspects of RDS.

RDS can be described as an Internal Review Board (IRB)–friendly recruitment strategy. This is especially important when working with hard-to-identify or hard-to-reach populations, since IRBs are responsible for being sensitive to protections for human subjects. With RDS, the researchers are not directly contacting members of a potentially at-risk population; instead, the members are being referred to the researcher and have the choice about whether to be identified as part of the population in the first place. As such, IRBs are more likely to approve of this sampling strategy (Heckathorn, 1997).

RDS is an innovative strategy for sampling hard-to-reach and hard-to-identify populations that, in the past, would have often gone without studies using representative samples.

Quota Sampling

Quota sampling is the nonprobability sampling method counterpart to stratified random sampling. It works in much the same way, except, of course, that a quota sample is not random and not a probability sample. While not random, a quota sample can guarantee that attributes/categories of key variables are represented in the sample. For instance, if sampling college students, a quota sample (with quotas for gender and race/ethnicity) could ensure that the sample maintains the same proportions of gender and race/ethnicity as the intended population. This goes a long way toward obtaining a representative sample. The more variables/categories used, the better that representativeness.

Moreover, quota sampling can be combined with other nonprobability sampling methods to add a dimension of representativeness, or a guarantee of representativeness along the lines of a particular variable or variables. Quotas can be set in tandem with the snowball sampling technique or even RDS.

Validating a Sample

Especially in the case of a nonrandom sample, it is important that efforts are made to validate the sample, to demonstrate that the sample is representative of the population. While not random, nonprobability samples that are representative can serve as powerful data from which to make predictions or draw conclusions about a population.

This can be done by testing demographic breakdowns on a sample and a population: average age, gender composition, racial/ethnic distribution, and so on. Depending on the research question or population, it may also be important to use other variables. If sampling from a college or university, you may want to validate class level or major, as well as whether students live on campus or off campus.

Validating the sample is best done using more than one variable to ensure that the sample is representative. Using only one demographic variable shows only one dimension of representativeness. On the other hand, after a handful of demographic variables for most populations, there are diminishing returns for adding additional variables to the validation list.

Split Ballot Designs

The General Social Survey, introduced in Chapter 1, uses a split ballot in order to maximize the amount of variables that can be used. The General Social Survey is a massive biannual survey research project. If each respondent were asked all of the questions, covering all of the variables in this survey, many would no doubt fall asleep or run screaming before the end of the questionnaire was reached.

The National Opinion Research Center, which administers the General Social Survey, asks some of the questions from the survey in only a random subsample of the households while asking other questions in other households. This can only be done since the General Social Survey sample in any given year typically consists of more than 2,000 respondents. Any baseline questions, such as demographics, remain among the questionnaires for all respondents (Wagner, 2016).

To be used only with relatively large samples, the split ballot design is effective at increasing the number of variables you can use in a survey without risking survey fatigue among respondents.

How and Where Are Data Collected Today?

While technology related to survey research used to be restricted to telephone and computer-assisted telephone interviewing software, there has been an immense increase in capabilities in computer hardware and Internet access speed/bandwidth, as well as access to the Internet in general. Most, not all, Americans are able to access the Internet in one or multiple ways. In the recent past, this was not the case. Today, many access the Internet via a smartphone or a tablet as well. This mobile access to the Internet has also introduced new possibilities along with challenges for data collection (and sampling methodologies). Software like Survey Monkey and Qualtrics allows for quite sophisticated survey design that, on the user end, can be graphical and interactive in nature (Ruel, Wagner, & Gillespie, 2015).

What was formerly a world of largely telephone and U.S. post office mail surveys has been quickly transformed primarily to the electronic (Internet and mobile) realm.

Terms

census 27
cluster sampling 30
convenience sampling 32
disproportionate stratified
   sampling 30
intended (target) population 27
nonprobability sample 31
periodicity 28
probability sample 27

proportionate stratified
   sampling 30
quota sampling 34
respondent-driven sampling 33
simple random sample 27
snowball sampling 32
stratified sampling 30
systematic random sampling 28

References

Heckathorn, D. (1997). Respondent-driven sampling: A new approach to the study of hidden populations. *Social Problems, 44*(2), 174–199.

Heckathorn, D. (2011). Comment: Snowball versus respondent driven sampling. *Sociological Methodology, 41*(1), 355–366.

Ruel, E., Wagner, W., & Gillespie, B. (2015). *The practice of survey research: Theory and applications.* Thousand Oaks, CA: Sage.

Wagner, W. (2016). *Using SPSS Statistics for research methods and social science statistics* (6th ed.). Thousand Oaks, CA: Sage.

Data Frequencies and Distributions

Univariate Frequencies and Relative Frequencies

Once a research topic has been chosen, measures have been tested and validated, and data have been collected from a target population, researchers then begin the process of data management and analysis. One of the first steps in hypothesis testing is to examine the variability, or heterogeneity, in the data. **Variability** is the amount of variation in individuals' scores for a given variable. If everyone scores the same on a given variable, it would be impossible to locate other factors that influence that variable. Take, for example, the hypothesis that more close friendships (friends) will lead to greater life satisfaction (lifesatis); if all individuals reported the same exact degree of life satisfaction, then it would be impossible to examine whether close friendships are associated with higher or lower satisfaction. Therefore, a first step is to explore variability in the data.

Table 4.1 shows how the data appear within a database for only 25 individuals. The first column, idnum, contains individuals' identification number. Each additional column represents a single measurement. For example, column 4 is titled "marstat," which uses an arbitrary number to indicate whether a participant has never been married (1) or is currently married (2), divorced (3), separated (4), or widowed (5). Given the complex list of scores in column 2, it would be extremely difficult to determine how many divorced individuals are in the sample by simply eyeballing the full list of scores. It is especially difficult when the sample size is large, arbitrary numerical codes represent nominal variables, and/or there is a wide range of possible scores.

TABLE 4.1 ● Numerically Coded Data Representing Demographic Information for 25 Individuals

idnum	age	sex	Marstat	Educ
466	33	0	2	5
575	34	0	1	3
651	30	1	2	4
666	51	1	2	3
693	58	0	4	3
694	48	0	2	4
730	30	1	1	5
737	32	1	2	5
738	45	1	3	3
747	50	0	3	3
750	52	1	4	3
753	47	1	2	5
796	25	1	1	4
830	38	0	2	4
867	66	1	3	4
900	56	1	2	5
916	26	1	1	5
990	37	1	2	5
994	51	1	2	4
996	38	0	2	4
1001	60	0	2	4
1049	42	1	3	4
1080	48	1	2	4
1085	62	1	3	4
1121	59	0	3	5

In order to look at the data in a more comprehensible way, researchers examine **frequency tables**, which are summary tables that indicate how observed scores are distributed across the sample population. These tables usually include information about frequencies, relative frequencies, percentages, cumulative percentages, and missing values. Importantly, in order to determine frequencies for a variable, the measurement must be constructed in such a way that the categories are both exhaustive and mutually exclusive. These two properties of variables are discussed in Chapter 2.

TABLE 4.2 ● Frequency Breakdown for Marital Status (`marstat`) With Information for Absolute Frequency, Relative Frequency, Full Percent, and Valid Percent					
Marital Status (`marstat`)					
		Absolute Frequency	**Relative Frequency**	**Full Percent**	**Valid Percent**
Valid	Never married	212	.21	21.2	21.2
	Married	617	.62	61.7	61.7
	Divorced	117	.12	11.7	11.7
	Separated	27	.27	2.7	2.7
	Widowed	27	.27	2.7	2.7
	Total	1,000	1	100.0	100.0

Table 4.2 illustrates the frequencies for marital status ("`marstat`") among a nonrandom sample of 1,000 U.S. adults.[1] **Absolute frequencies** provide the counts for each attribute of a variable. In this table, we can see that there are 617 married individuals in the sample. Since this is the marital status category with the highest frequency, it is also the modal category. However, an absolute frequency does not provide information about the frequency in the context of the whole sample—as a part of a whole.

Relative frequencies provide a proportional measure of each category relative to the total sample. These summary statistics are conventionally presented in the form of **percentages**. In order to convert relative frequencies into percentages, just multiply the proportion by 100. In the "relative frequency" column of the same table, the proportion of individuals in the sample who are married is .617, and the proportion for never married is .212. Therefore, 62% of individuals in the sample are married and 21% have never been married. The remaining 17% is made up of those individuals who are divorced, separated, or widowed.

Frequency tables also include the number of cases that have missing information for the variable under investigation. As a result, percentages can be interpreted in different ways depending on how the missing data are handled. When calculating percentages, the **full percentage** includes all cases in the sample size—even those with missing values. On the other hand, the **valid percentage** is the percentage of individuals with a given value based on a sample size that *excludes* cases with missing values. For example, a professor

---

[1] The data used in analyses for this chapter are based on a nonrandom Internet sample of U.S. adults ($N = 1,000$).

teaching a course with 100 students enrolled is interested in knowing how diverse the course is across the different class cohorts. At the start of class one morning, she asks each student to identify his or her grade level. The frequency distribution is 15 freshmen, 15 sophomores, 24 juniors, and 26 seniors—20 students were absent that day.

The professor notes that the *full* percentage of juniors in the course is less than a quarter (24%) when the sample size ($N = 100$) includes those 20 students who were absent. However, when the sample is comprised of only those students who were present ($N = 80$), juniors make up 30% of the class. In most cases (including this one), the valid percentage is arguably more informative since information about the absent students—aside from their enrollment—is unknown.

Cumulative Percentages and Percentiles

Although researchers commonly report relative frequencies to show the proportion of individuals with a specific score, when data are ordinal or interval/ratio, they can be interpreted in relation to their placement on an ordered scale. **Cumulative frequencies** provide an additive summary of frequencies up to and including a given category. Similarly, **cumulative percentages** provide the summary of accumulated percentages—the percentage with a given attribute plus all the preceding attributes.

Table 4.3 presents a frequency table for highest level of education completed (educ). The full percentage indicates that 32.2% ($n = 322$) of individuals

TABLE 4.3 ● Frequency Breakdown for Level of Education (educ) With Information for Absolute Frequency, Relative Frequency, Full Percent, Cumulative Frequency, and Cumulative Percent					
Level of Education (educ)					
		Absolute Frequency	Relative Frequency	Full Percent	Cumulative Frequency	Cumulative Percent
Valid	Less than high school	5	.005	.5	5	.5
	High school	81	.08	8.1	86	8.6
	Some college or AA	309	.31	30.9	395	39.5
	College degree	322	.32	32.2	717	71.7
	Postgraduate degree	283	.28	28.3	1,000	100.0
	Total	1,000	1	100.0		

in the sample have a college degree. However, in order to ascertain how many people have a college degree *or below*, a cumulative percentage is necessary. The information in the table shows a cumulative percentage of 71.1% for college degree. This means that 71% of individuals in the sample have a college education *or below*.

Cumulative percentages are also known as **percentile ranks** because they show where values fall within the ordered set of cumulative percentages. For example, Table 4.4 presents a frequency table for self-rated physical attraction (srattract) among a nonrandom sample of 1,000 U.S. adults. The ordered scale, which ranges from 1–10, is based on the following prompt: "Compared to most people my age, I would say that I am. . . ." The response options range from (1) *extremely unattractive* to (10) *extremely attractive*. The attribute "average" has a percentile rank (i.e., cumulative percent) of 35.1%. Therefore, an individual who reports being "average" in physical appearance falls in the 35th percentile for self-reported attractiveness. The individual's reported attractiveness is greater than or equal to 35% of the sample. As discussed later in Chapter 6, the median is the 50th percentile—that is, the middle of the ordered distribution is a self-rated attractiveness of 6.

TABLE 4.4 ● Frequency Breakdown for Self-Reported Attractiveness (srattract) With Information for Absolute Frequency, Relative Frequency, Full Percent, Cumulative Frequency, and Cumulative Percent

	Self-Rated Physical Attractiveness Scale (srattract)				
		Absolute Frequency	Relative Frequency	Full Percent	Cumulative Frequency	Cumulative Percent
Valid	Extremely unattractive	5	.005	.5	5	.5
	2	10	.01	1.0	15	1.5
	3	25	.03	2.5	40	4.0
	4	41	.04	4.1	81	8.1
	Average	270	.27	27.0	351	35.1
	6	165	.17	16.5	516	51.6
	7	211	.21	21.1	727	72.7
	8	187	.19	18.7	914	91.4
	9	60	.06	6.0	974	97.4
	Extremely attractive	26	.03	2.6	1,000	100.0
	Total	1,000	1	100.0		

TABLE 4.5 ● Frequency Breakdown for Marital Status (`marstat`), Including Cumulative Percentage

		Absolute Frequency	Relative Frequency	Full Percent	Valid Percent	Cumulative Percent
	Marital Status (marstat)					
Valid	Never married	212	.21	21.2	21.2	21.2
	Married	617	.62	61.7	61.7	82.9
	Divorced	117	.12	11.7	11.7	94.6
	Separated	27	.27	2.7	2.7	97.3
	Widowed	27	.27	2.7	2.7	100
	Total	1,000	1	100.0	100.0	

Although cumulative frequencies or percentages are sometimes presented in statistical output, it would not be intuitive to interpret them for a nominal variable. Since these variables do not have a logical ordering, a cumulative interpretation would be incorrect and unclear. For example, Table 4.5 presents cumulative percentages for the variable `marstat`. It would not make sense to suggest that 94.6% of individuals are divorced *or less* because marital status has no logical rank ordering—there is no "less than divorce."

One important point to keep in mind when interpreting cumulative percentages is whether or not the ordinal categories are ascending from the lowest to the highest values—as with the last example—or descending from the highest to lowest values. If the information above were presented in reverse fashion in a frequency table, the interpretation would be different. Using a reverse-coded `srattractrev` variable that descends from 1 (*extremely attractive*) to 10 (*least attractive*), the attribute for average is 64.9. In this (reversed) case, 65% of individuals in the sample report being average *or more* attractive.

Frequencies for Quantitative Data

Interpreting frequency distributions for quantitative data is a more difficult process because these variables often have a large number of possible scores. Table 4.6 presents only a partial frequency table for the variable `age`. A simplified way of presenting and interpreting quantitative variables in frequency tables is to use **grouped frequencies**. Grouped frequencies collapse the interval/ratio data into a smaller number of groups based on the researcher's interest in different groups.

Table 4.7 presents a frequency table for age that looks at frequencies within different age groups (`agegroup`). In this table, age is presented in an ordered

TABLE 4.6 ● Frequency Distribution for the Variable age

		Frequency Distribution for age			
Age	Frequency	Age	Frequency	Age	Frequency
18	4	38	26	58	17
19	9	39	28	59	11
20	12	40	22	60	14
21	12	41	20	61	15
22	13	42	20	62	19
23	14	43	26	63	8
24	20	44	29	64	9
25	26	45	34	65	8
26	20	46	24	66	9
27	18	47	32	67	6
28	22	48	20	68	3
29	23	49	38	69	6
30	29	50	34	70	5
31	21	51	27	71	1
32	21	52	30	72	1
33	27	53	16	73	3
34	22	54	21	74	3
35	23	55	11	75	7
36	10	56	10	Total	1,000
37	16	57	25		

TABLE 4.7 ● Grouped Frequencies for the Variable agegroup

Age Group (agegroup)					
	Absolute Frequency	Relative Frequency	Full Percent	Cumulative Frequency	Cumulative Percent
Early adulthood (18–34)	313	.31	31.3	313	31.3
Adulthood (35–64)	635	.64	63.5	948	94.8
Older adulthood (65+)	52	.05	5.2	1,000	100.0
Total	1,000	1	100.0		

group of categories without consistent intervals, making it an interval/ratio variable that was transformed into an ordinal variable. However, the grouped frequencies facilitate interpretation of the age distribution based on these categories. The sample is largely made up of individuals in midlife adulthood, between the ages of 35 and 64 (63.5%)—this is also the modal age category ($n = 635$). Early adults ages 18 to 34 make up 31.3% of the sample, and just over 5% are age 65 and over. Another way to interpret the distribution of interval/ratio-level data is by looking at the distribution in a histogram.

Univariate Distributions

A common way to explore variability across different attributes of the data is to visually explore the distribution. A histogram represents the distribution of interval/ratio scores—it is helpful for researchers looking to visually examine the shape, variation, and center of a frequency distribution. In a histogram, the *x*-axis (horizontal) represents the scores for a given interval/ratio variable. The *y*-axis (vertical) represents the frequencies in which the scores occur in the data.[2]

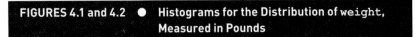

FIGURES 4.1 and 4.2 ● Histograms for the Distribution of weight, Measured in Pounds

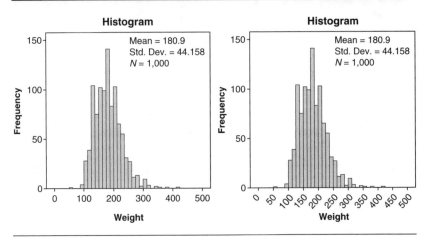

Note: The histogram in the left panel (Figure 4.1) has intervals of 100 units. The histogram in the right panel (Figure 4.2) has intervals of 50 units.

---

[2] Several other terms are used to identify the *x*- and *y*-axes:

- **x-axis**: Abscissa, Horizontal Axis
- **y-axis**: Ordinate, Vertical Axis

Figure 4.1 presents a histogram of `weight` ($N = 1,000$). The intervals are presented in clusters of 100 units. As such, the frequency of individuals with weight between 100 and 200 pounds is represented between those markers on the x-axis. The scale on the x-axis can be changed to represent other smaller or larger intervals—the shape of the distribution does not change. Figure 4.2 presents the same histogram with intervals of 50 instead of 100. This figure also includes a smoothed line that captures the general shape of the distribution's curve. In order to compare the histogram's distribution to a theoretical model, researchers draw on a theoretical frequency curve known as the normal distribution.

The Normal Distribution

The normal distribution, also called the normal curve, bell curve, or Gaussian distribution, is a theoretical "standard" distribution that researchers use to approximately parallel the frequency distribution of their variables. Since the normal curve is a theoretical distribution, researchers do not expect data to align perfectly with the bell-shaped normal distribution—but the model is used to approximate the "normality" of their data. However, over time and additional observations, most distributions in the natural and social sciences do approach an approximately normal distribution. This is known as the **central limit theorem**. In order to interpret and approximate a histogram distribution vis-à-vis the normal curve, researchers focus on a number of characteristics: the peak, the tails, and the shoulders.

Characteristics of the Normal Distribution

Figure 4.3 presents a diagram of the normal distribution. The base of the distribution is the x-axis marked with intervals for the variable. The y-axis

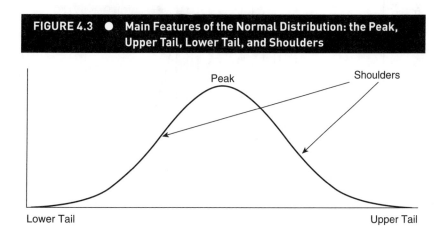

FIGURE 4.3 ● Main Features of the Normal Distribution: the Peak, Upper Tail, Lower Tail, and Shoulders

Peak

Shoulders

Lower Tail   Upper Tail represents the height, or distribution for each unit. The **peak** of the normal distribution is the highest point—there is only one such point, making the normal distribution a **unimodal** one. The **tails** are the areas to the left extreme, the **lower tail**, and the right extreme, the **upper tail**. The distribution is also **symmetrical**, meaning that the left half is a mirror image of the right half and 50% of the distribution lies in each half. Most of the distribution lies in the middle area, and it decreases as it curves toward the tails.

Figure 4.4 presents a histogram for height in inches (height) using the same data with an overlay representing the shape of the normal curve. As the central limit theorem posits, the inclusion of additional observations of individuals' height would lead the distribution to more precisely approximate a normal curve, whereby smaller numbers of extremely short and extremely tall

FIGURE 4.4   ●   Histogram for the Distribution of height, Measured in Inches, With the Normal Curve Overlaid

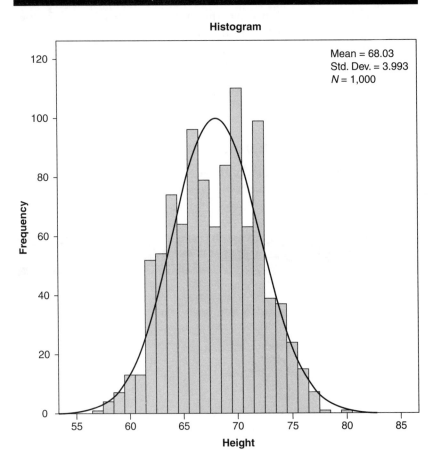

individuals will be in the left and right tails, respectively. Most of the distribution would tend toward the middle—with a single peak at the central point.

Normal Quantile-Quantile Plots

Another way to assess the normality of a distribution is to examine a **normal quantile-quantile plot**. The normal quantile-quantile plot, also known as a normal probability plot or a Q-Q plot, presents a visualization of how the distribution of scores for a variable compares to what one would expect in a normal distribution. Figure 4.5 presents a normal quantile-quantile plot for the variable `height`. In this plot, the circles represent the observed scores for the sample population. The line indicates where we would expect scores to land if the data were normally distributed. Thus, based on how closely the observed values (circles) match the theoretical normal distribution (solid line), researchers can assess where values deviate from a normal distribution.

FIGURE 4.5   ●   A Normal Q-Q Plot for the Variable `height`

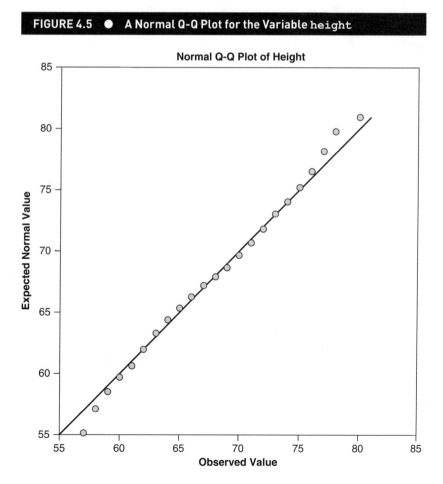

Non-Normal Distribution Characteristics

When examining the distribution of interval/ratio variables, researchers often find that there are aspects of the distribution that are unlike the normal curve. The next section discusses these issues, particularly as they relate to multimodality, skewness, and kurtosis.

Bimodal and Multimodal Distributions

As discussed earlier, the modal score is the score with the highest frequency. Accordingly, the normal distribution has only a single central point (i.e., a "tower"). However, distributions sometimes have two peaks (**bimodal distributions**), which can occur if the distribution is made up of two groups with different characteristics. Take, for example, the Department of Psychology at Sage University. The department is interested in collecting data on student performance in statistics courses one semester. If the data it collects produce a bimodal distribution, it might mean that two different populations were included in the distribution. If, for example, there were two different instructors for the course, each with different teaching styles and examinations, then the distribution of scores might be a reflection of different course instructors, resulting in bimodality. Less commonly, there are more than two peaks, which indicates that there is a **multimodal distribution**. The panels in Figure 4.6 illustrate a normal distribution (a), a bimodal distribution (b), and a multimodal distribution (c).

Skewness

The shape of a distribution can be influenced by **skewness** in the scores. Skewness is sometimes linked to **outliers** in the data, which are extreme scores that cause a directional bias toward the left or right. The direction of a skew is based on the side that extends farther and creates a "tail." When there are fewer values on the left side and distribution of scores is aggregated on the right side, then the tail is on the left side—this is a **negatively skewed** distribution. On the other hand, if there are fewer scores on the right side, the distribution is **positively skewed**. Examples of negatively and positively skewed distributions are presented in Figure 4.7.

FIGURE 4.6 ● Panels Illustrating Distributions That Are (a) Unimodal, (b) Bimodal, and (c) Multimodal

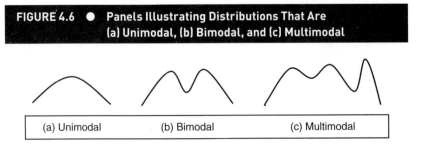

(a) Unimodal   (b) Bimodal   (c) Multimodal

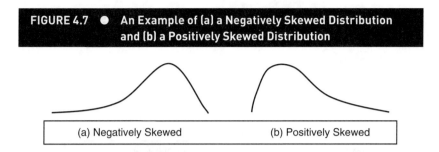

FIGURE 4.7 ● An Example of (a) a Negatively Skewed Distribution and (b) a Positively Skewed Distribution

| (a) Negatively Skewed | (b) Positively Skewed |

TABLE 4.8 ● Distribution Characteristics for the Variable height

height (in.)		
N	Valid	1,000
	Missing	0
Skewness (a)		−.041
Std. error of skewness (b)		.077
Excess kurtosis (c)		−.583
Std. error of excess kurtosis (d)		.155

Researchers use statistical metrics to assess the normality of given distributions. These values also provide some indication about the direction of a non-normal variable distribution. The value for skewness indicates the distribution's symmetry, with the baseline symmetry of a normal distribution represented as zero. When interpreting the coefficient for skewness, any deviation from zero describes the direction and magnitude of asymmetry, or skewness. If the value of skewness is positive, then the distribution is positively skewed; if the value is negative, then the data are negatively skewed. Based on the information provided in Table 4.8, individuals' height is skewed negatively because the coefficient for skewness (a) is less than zero.

There is no strict cutoff for what is considered to be an unacceptably high or low skewness value. One commonly accepted approach for examining the magnitude of non-normality is to divide the skewness value by its respective standard error and compare it to an approximate range of −1.9 to 1.9. If the result falls outside of that range, the distribution is considered non-normal. Thus, the information in Table 4.8 can also help determine if the distribution deviates substantially from a normal distribution. The skewness value (−.041) can be divided by the standard error of skewness (b), which is .077. This yields a value of −0.53. Since this value lands within the acceptable −1.9 to 1.9 range, the distribution would not be considered a substantially skewed deviation from the normal distribution.

Kurtosis

Kurtosis indicates how concentrated the scores are around a central tendency. As such, it points to how flat a distribution is based on its tails and peak

FIGURE 4.8 ● A Leptokurtic and a Platykurtic Distribution

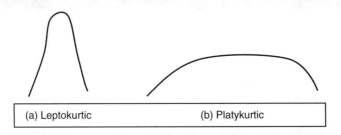

(a) Leptokurtic   (b) Platykurtic

(see Figure 4.8). A normal curve has a **mesokurtic distribution**. A flatter distribution is known as a **platykurtic distribution**, whereas a **leptokurtic distribution** has a pointier peak and steeper curve in the shoulders of the distribution. As with skewness, many statistical applications provide a metric for kurtosis that indicates how a given distribution compares to the normal distribution.

The numerical value of kurtosis is compared to the baseline value of kurtosis for a normal distribution, which is 3. Therefore, if the value for kurtosis is greater than 3, the distribution is leptokurtic. A kurtosis value less than 3 indicates that there is a platykurtic distribution. Some statistical software packages report the value of **excess kurtosis**, which subtracts 3 from the kurtosis value. This allows for kurtosis to be interpreted in a way similar to that of skewness—with a baseline value of zero. In this case, a negative number indicates that a distribution is platykurtic, and a positive number means that a distribution is leptokurtic. Therefore, in order to interpret the values of kurtosis from a given software package, it is necessary to determine which kurtosis value is presented.

The negative value for excess kurtosis (c) in Table 4.8 indicates that the distribution for height is platykurtic. Similar to the assessment of the magnitude of skewness, dividing the excess kurtosis score (–.583) by the standard error of kurtosis (d), which is .155, yields a value of –3.76. Since this value is outside of the range between –1.9 and 1.9, this suggests that the distribution for individuals' `height` is non-normal.

As a result of the arbitrary guidelines for interpretation of magnitude and differences in the coefficients provided by statistical packages, it is also strongly advised to use visual interpretation of normality or non-normality to confirm the results of the coefficients. There are several statistical procedures used to test for normality in data (e.g., Shapiro-Wilk and Kolmogorov-Smirnov) that are discussed in later chapters.

Data Transformations for Dealing With Non-Normal Distributions

Researchers commonly employ methods to "transform" non-normal distributions into more normal approximations. This process often requires taking a mathematical conversion of scores in order to "normalize" them. For example, when skewed scores violate the assumptions of normality, researchers take the natural log of the variable in order to change the shape and make the distribution more symmetrical. Figure 4.9a presents a histogram with information on the 2000 county population for 1,000 U.S. adults (countypop). The data are clearly non-normal, and the skewness and kurtosis values in Table 4.9 confirm this. However, as Figure 4.9b and the second part of Table 4.9 indicate, taking the natural log of the variable (countylog) "normalizes" the distribution.

A full discussion of the ways researchers deal with non-normal distributions is outside of the scope of this book; however, it is important to note that *these transformations change the interpretation of data.* As such, researchers must be cautious when presenting and interpreting results based on transformed data.

FIGURE 4.9 ● Two Histograms for County Population

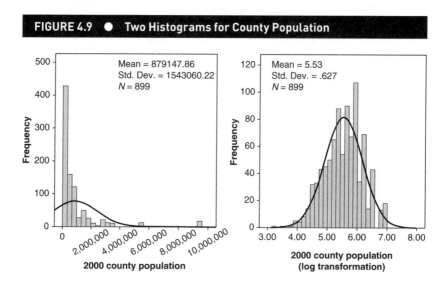

TABLE 4.9 ● Distribution Characteristics for County Population (countypop) and the Log Transformation of County Population (countylog)

Distribution Characteristics		2000 County Population	Log of 2000 County Population
N	Valid	899	899
	Missing	101	101
Skewness		3.981	−.175
Std. error of skewness		.082	.082
Excess kurtosis		18.116	−.105
Std. error of excess kurtosis		.163	.163

Bivariate Frequencies

Now that we have explored how to look at frequency distributions for a single variable (univariate frequencies), it is time to turn to the exploration of the relationship between two or more variables. As Chapter 2 discussed, hypotheses are testable statements about the relationship between variables. As a first step in looking at how these relationships play out in the data, researchers examine bivariate **contingency tables**—also known as crosstabulation tables or crosstabs. Contingency tables are frequencies and/or percentages of one variable tabulated separately across different categories of a second variable. They show the frequency breakdown of categories in one variable as they are *contingent upon* values of another variable.

An example of this would be a researcher who is interested in exploring whether friends cause stress (stressfriends) separately for men and women (sex). Because both variables are nominal and dichotomous, they are each represented by arbitrary numerical codes in the data. In the variable sex, the code for *male* is "0," and the code for *female* is "1." The variable stressfriends is based on the following question: "Does your relationship with your friends bring you a lot of stress?" The numerical codes assigned to these responses are "0" for *no* and "1" for *yes*. Table 4.10 presents a contingency table for these variables. In this table, we identify sex as the independent variable and happiness as the dependent variable. By convention, researchers put the independent variable on top (the categories are represented by **columns**) and the dependent variable is on the left (represented in the **rows**). The boxes in the table that provide individual frequencies and percentages are known as **cells**. The cells give the value of one variable across different categories of another.

The cells that are located in the sidelines of a contingency table are known as the **margins**. Margins are the totals for a given category of a variable and are therefore essentially the same as exploring a frequency table for that variable, based on whether it is presented in the row or column. The modal response for the dependent variable is presented in the **row margins**. Therefore, in Table 4.10, we are able to say that most individuals in the sample—regardless

---

TABLE 4.10 ● Contingency Table for sex and stressfriends (raw frequencies [counts] only)

stressfriends * sex Contingency Table				
		Sex		
		Male	Female	Total
Relationship with friends brings a lot of stress	No	500	431	931
	Yes	23	46	69
Total		523	477	1,000

of their sex—reported that their friends *do not* cause them a lot of stress. Given that 931 individuals reported that their friends do not cause them a lot of stress compared to only 69 who said that they do, we have identified the modal category for the dependent variable. Similarly, the **column margins** indicate that the modal category for the independent variable is male ($n = 523$) as opposed to 477 women. The cells inside of the margins represent the crosstabulated data on stressfriends for men and women separately.

While the raw numbers can tell us the modal response and point to some other interesting trends, the data in a contingency table must be interpreted using percentages in order to draw meaningful comparisons. If one were to interpret differences between men and women based on the raw frequencies, the comparisons would be susceptible to different sample sizes for the groups. For example, if there are more men in the sample, then it might appear in the frequencies that more men than women report being stressed by their friends— but this might merely be a reflection of the fact that the sample consists of more men than women. Therefore, researchers *must interpret the percentages across each category*.

The frequency in every cell can be converted into two percentages based on its proportion to a whole. However, the "whole" that we are talking about varies according to the variable and its placement. Since sex is the independent variable in this example, the contingency table (Table 4.11) presents percentages of stressfriends for men and women independently—in this case, we explore the **column percentages**. Column percentages identify percentages for each response in the row variable for the full sample of men and the full sample of women. Therefore, these percentages add up to 100% for men and 100% for women in the column margins.

With this table, a researcher is able to explore differences in the percentages of men and women within each category of stressfriends. For instance,

TABLE 4.11 ● Contingency Table for sex and stressfriends With *Column* Percentages

stressfriends * sex Contingency Table					
			Male	Female	Total
Relationship with friends brings a lot of stress	No	Count	500	431	931
		% within sex	95.6%	90.4%	93.1%
	Yes	Count	23	46	69
		% within sex	4.4%	9.6%	6.9%
Total		Count	523	477	1,000
		% within sex	100.0%	100.0%	100.0%

if the same percentages of women and men report feeling stressed by their friends, that is a strong indication that the two are pretty similar. One way to quickly spot similarities and differences between two groups is to take one category as a reference and compare the other group by subtracting the percentage. In this example, we can subtract the stressfriends percentage for males from the percentage for females. Thus, there is a difference of 5.2 percentage points between men and women on stressfriends (9.6 – 4.4).

As with all data interpretations, a main objective is to take a complicated series of units or numbers and present a boiled-down version of the most interesting identifiable patterns. One possible interpretation of these numbers is that "of the women in the sample, 9.6% reported feeling very stressed out by their friends, compared to 4.4% of men." Put more simply, a researcher could say, "A higher percentage of women than men reported that their friends cause a lot of stress in their lives."

It is also possible to review and interpret row percentages in contingency tables (see Table 4.12). **Row percentages** indicate what percent of each stressfriends category consists of males and females. These percentages *are not the same values as column percentages* because now we are exploring percentages across the stressfriends groups rather than across sex categories. This is illustrated in the table with *row margins* that add up to 100%. Interpretation of this table is based on a different subset of people—rather than exploring *all women*, we are now looking at the group *individuals who reported stress with their friends* instead. This interpretation is a bit different: "Of those who reported that their relationship with their friends causes them a lot of stress, the majority (66.7%) were women."

TABLE 4.12 ●   Contingency Table for sex and stressfriends With *Row* **Percentages**

stressfriends * sex Contingency Table				Sex		
				Male	Female	Total
Relationship with friends brings a lot of stress	No	Count		500	431	931
		% within relationship with friends brings a lot of stress		53.7%	46.3%	100.0%
	Yes	Count		23	46	69
		% within relationship with friends brings a lot of stress		33.3%	66.7%	100.0%
Total		Count		523	477	1,000
		% within relationship with friends brings a lot of stress		52.3%	47.7%	100.0%

In this example, several different questions can be answered based on (a) which variable is in the row and which is in the column and (b) whether or not the interpretation is based on column percentages or row percentages. Column percentages are necessary in order to answer the following questions:

Question: Of all men in the sample, what percentage are stressed by their friends?

Answer: 4.4%

Question: Of all women in the sample, what percentage are stressed by their friends?

Answer: 9.6%

Question: Of all males in the sample, what percentage are not stressed by their friends?

Answer: 95.6%

Question: Of all females in the sample, what percentage are not stressed by their friends?

Answer: 90.4%

On the other hand, row percentages help to answer these fundamentally different questions:

Question: Of all individuals who are stressed by their friends, what percentage are male?

Answer: 33.3%

Question: Of all individuals who are stressed by their friends, what percentage are female?

Answer: 66.7%

Question: Of those who are not stressed by their friends, what percentage are male?

Answer: 53.7%

Question: Of those who are not stressed by their friends, what percentage are female?

Answer: 46.3%

These two sets of questions yield different results because they are based on different subsets in the sample. Based on convention, it is generally recommended to interpret differences in column percentages because they show differences across the independent variable.

Table 4.13 presents an example of a contingency table with three categories for the independent variable. This table presents frequencies for `stressfriends` across different categorizations of sexual orientation (`sorient`). Based on the raw numbers, it might appear that heterosexuals are far more likely than gay/lesbian and bisexual individuals to report stress with their friendships. That is because the raw numbers are misleading—they reflect the fact that there are more heterosexual than gay/lesbian and bisexual individuals in the sample. Therefore, in order to accurately explore differences across sexual orientation groups, column percentages are necessary (Table 4.14).

In the table with column percentages, it becomes more apparent that there are some noteworthy differences in `stressfriends` across sexual orientation

TABLE 4.13 ● **Contingency Table for the Variables stressfriends and sorient (raw frequencies [counts] only)**

stressfriends * sorient Contingency Table					
		Sexual Orientation			
		Heterosexual	**Gay/Lesbian**	**Bisexual**	**Total**
Relationship with friends brings a lot of stress	No	881	26	24	931
	Yes	63	4	2	69
Total		944	30	26	1,000

TABLE 4.14 ● **Contingency Table for the Variables stressfriends and sorient With *Column* Percentages**

stressfriends * sorient Contingency Table						
			Sexual Orientation			
			Heterosexual	**Gay/Lesbian**	**Bisexual**	**Total**
Relationship with friends brings a lot of stress	No	Count	881	26	24	931
		% within sexual orientation	93.3%	86.7%	92.3%	93.1%
	Yes	Count	63	4	2	69
		% within sexual orientation	6.7%	13.3%	7.7%	6.9%
Total		Count	944	30	26	1,000
		% within sexual orientation	100.0%	100.0%	100.0%	100.0%

categories. In particular, bisexual and heterosexual individuals appear similar—and gay men and lesbians have higher reports of stress with their friendships. Of course, this is likely to be the result of the very small number of gay, lesbian, and bisexual individuals in the sample, generally, and reporting stress with their friendships, in particular.

There are a variety of different approaches to presenting and interpreting contingency tables in a more advanced way. For example, later chapters discuss the inclusion of a third variable to look at how different bivariate relationships change for different groups. Additionally, since ordinal variables have additional information about ordered categories, researchers can explore the direction of different relationships. These ideas are discussed in later chapters as they relate to the official testing of hypotheses. For now, the basics are important for understanding the breakdown of a variable's categories across the categories of another variable—this helps you look for relationships in a preliminary way.

Conclusion

As noted previously, researchers are concerned with the amount of variability in their data. As such, they pay close attention to frequency distributions for nominal and ordinal data. These indicate the degree to which individuals score across a variety of possibilities. It is also important to focus on visual and numerical aspects of distributions for interval/ratio variables. These interpretations are based on comparison to a theoretical model, the normal distribution. In order to explore relationships between two (or more) variables, researchers interpret contingency tables that display the percentage of the independent variable across different categories of the dependent variable. In addition to the procedures in this chapter, a variety of charts and graphs allow researchers to easily interpret the distribution of scores and bivariate relationships between variables. These data visualizations are the focus of the next chapter.

Terms

absolute frequencies 39	cumulative percentages 40
bimodal distributions 48	excess kurtosis 50
cells 52	frequency tables 38
central limit theorem 45	full percentage 39
column margins 53	grouped frequencies 42
column percentages 53	kurtosis 49
columns 52	leptokurtic distribution 50
contingency tables 52	lower tail 46
cumulative frequencies 40	margins 52

(Continued)

(Continued)

mesokurtic distribution 50	relative frequencies 39
multimodal distribution 48	row margins 52
negatively skewed 48	row percentages 54
normal quantile-quantile	rows 52
plots 47	skewness 48
outliers 48	symmetrical 46
peak 46	tails 46
percentages 39	unimodal 46
percentile ranks 41	upper tail 46
platykurtic distribution 50	valid percentage 39
positively skewed 48	variability 37

Using and Interpreting Univariate and Bivariate Visualizations

Before beginning formal statistical analysis, researchers can tell a great deal about their data by interpreting charts and graphs. Like frequency tables discussed in the previous chapter, data visualization is the process of taking many data points and presenting them in a way that is interpretable. This chapter discusses how to interpret some of the most common types of charts and graphs. This is important because data are sometimes presented in misleading ways (sometimes on purpose but other times because of poor understanding of the ways data can/should be presented). Therefore, we also explicitly discuss common ways that data visualizations can be misinterpreted. This is so you can (a) avoid these pitfalls in your own research and (b) assess other visualizations to determine if they are effectively displaying information that represents the data.

At the outset, a researcher must choose an appropriate way to present the data visually—this is usually based on the level of variable measurement. Once a technique has been established, a researcher presenting data in visual form must establish *what he or she is trying to convey*. The use of graphs and charts differs based on the information being presented (the story you want to tell). Similar to the distributions discussed in Chapter 4, data visualizations vary in their usefulness depending on whether a researcher is interested in presenting data in absolute terms, relative terms, or cumulatively. In this way, charts and graphs are useful for telling a visual story about patterns in the data—based on what you want to convey. However, if there is no story to tell, then a visual will likely be an ineffective tool.

Data can be presented in visual form for a single variable (univariate visualization), two variables (bivariate visualization), or multiple variables (multivariate visualization). This chapter focuses primarily on univariate and bivariate charts and graphs. One important concept linking most of the graphs and charts in this chapter are the horizontal (x) and vertical (y) axes, which are necessary for variable placement and interpretation. First, we turn to the two most common forms of univariate data visualization, bar charts and pie charts.

Univariate Data Visualization

Bar Graphs

Bar graphs, also known as simple bar charts, are a common way of visually presenting categorical (nominal, ordinal, and dichotomous) data. These charts are useful for showing absolute frequencies across multiple independent categories of a variable. As such, the columns in the chart are presented as independent categories with appropriate labels for each. The lines do not line up against each other as they do with histograms (see Chapter 4) because histograms represent quantitative (interval/ratio) data ranges with consistent intervals along the x-axis. Instead, bar charts show variation in the data frequencies for standalone categories. Figure 5.1 presents bar charts for marital status (`marstat`) from a sample of 1,000 men and women, illustrating the different frequencies across each category.

In the first panel of Figure 5.1, the frequencies are listed in the y-axis with tick marks in 200-unit frequency ranges. This bar graph is also sometimes

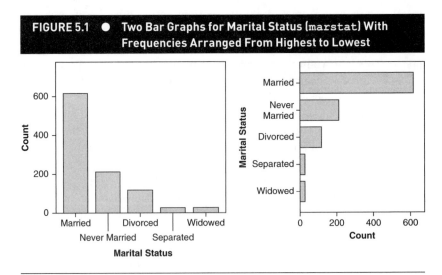

FIGURE 5.1 ● Two Bar Graphs for Marital Status (`marstat`) With Frequencies Arranged From Highest to Lowest

Note: The left panel shows the bars arranged vertically, and the right panel shows the bars arranged horizontally.

referred to as a vertical bar chart or a column chart. The vertical length of the bar represents the frequencies for each marital status category. In order to facilitate quick interpretation, the bars are usually arranged from highest to lowest frequency unless there is some other reason to order them differently. Even the quickest glance indicates that the modal category for the individuals in the sample is married, followed by never married, and then divorced. Given how similar they appear, frequencies were included with the bars representing separated and widowed individuals. Otherwise, in order to avoid redundancy and reduce clutter, the raw numbers are not necessary—unless, of course, they are important to effectively tell your story.

The second panel of Figure 5.1 shows a horizontal bar graph with the bars for the same marital status category frequencies arranged horizontally rather than vertically. The choice of whether the bars are presented horizontally (along the *x*-axis) or vertically (along the *y*-axis) is mostly a matter of personal preference—the use and interpretation is the same. Some argue that horizontal bar charts are easier to interpret since it is easier to quickly identify the endpoints. Moreover, the use of horizontal bars allows for longer names beyond the *y*-axis—so if each category has long titles, a horizontal chart might be the more appropriate option.

Presentation and Interpretation Issues

One of the most important issues regarding the misinterpretation of bar graph data is when the scale is manipulated to start at some baseline other than zero. This is known as a **truncated graph** because the graph is cut in order to have a baseline frequency above zero—and doing so manipulates the visual interpretation of the magnitude of the frequencies. For example, Figure 5.2 illustrates differences in the number of men and women in the sample of 1,000 adults. At first glance, it appears as though there are three times more men in the sample than women. However, note that the *x*-axis begins at 460. This truncated graph is misleading because the *x*-axis does not start with a baseline of zero—as such, the magnitude of difference appears much larger. On the other hand, Figure 5.3 presents frequencies for men and women in the sample with a baseline of zero—this demonstrates that, while there are more men than women in the sample, the difference is actually quite minimal.

Bar graphs are important for illustrating the frequencies for individual categories of a categorical variable. However, this type of data visualization does not tell us about the categories in relative terms, that is, the contribution of each category to the whole sample. Pie charts are a useful way to demonstrate relative frequencies and percentages.

Pie Charts

Although bar graphs and pie charts are sometimes used interchangeably to represent data visually, the two serve somewhat different purposes. The primary

FIGURE 5.2 ● Truncated Bar Chart Showing The Difference Between the Number of Men and Women in the Sample (sex)

Note: Note that the baseline on the x-axis begins at 460.

FIGURE 5.3 ● Bar Graph Using the Same Data for the Variable sex With the *x*-Axis Baseline Value at Zero

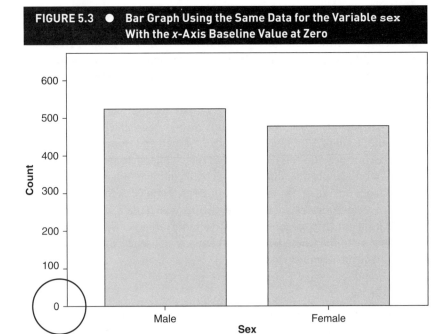

function of a **pie chart** is to visually demonstrate the relative frequency or percentage of each category in its relation to the whole sample.[1] Therefore, the most important feature of a pie chart is the relative contribution of individual sections, or "slices," to the whole pie. The area of each section determines its relative contribution to the full pie. Therefore, if one section gets bigger, others must get smaller—the composition of the pie chart depends upon the relative size of each section. In addition to the area of the pie taken up by each section, the angles for each section (where the lines intersect) provide insights into its relative contribution to the full proportion of responses.

The categories of a pie chart must total 100% of the full sample. As such, the sections of a pie chart must hold two important properties: They must be exhaustive and mutually exclusive. In order for the categories in a pie chart to be exhaustive, there must be representation for all categories represented by the variable. Table 5.1 presents the frequencies for marital status in the sample of 1,000 individuals. The pie chart in Figure 5.4 would not be an accurate representation of the relative frequencies for marital status because the chart reveals the contribution of only two of the categories, married and never married, to the full sample. In this regard, a pie chart is pointless because the totals do not add up to 1,000.

The sections represented in a pie chart must also be mutually exclusive, meaning that data points cannot be represented in more than one section of the pie. For example, Figure 5.5 presents a pie chart depicting individuals' report of which items cause them a lot of stress. Given that individuals were able to identify *multiple* items that cause stress (e.g., someone could choose both work *and* family), the resulting chart is not based on mutually exclusive categories. The count totals add up to more than 1,000, which is not an

TABLE 5.1 ● Frequencies for the Variable Marital Status (marstat), Including Information on Relative Frequencies and Percentages

Marital Status (marstat)		Absolute Frequency	Relative Frequency	Full Percent	Valid Percent
Valid	Never married	212	.21	21.2	21.2
	Married	617	.62	61.7	61.7
	Divorced	117	.12	11.7	11.7
	Separated	27	.27	2.7	2.7
	Widowed	27	.27	2.7	2.7
	Total	1,000	1	100.0	100.0

[1] Pie charts are also known as circle graphs or circular graphs. They are similar to donut charts, which are a more detailed way of presenting data.

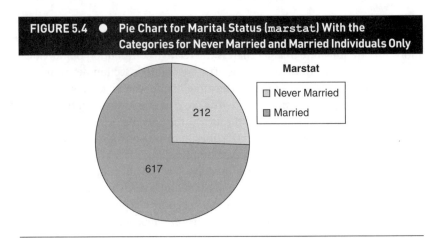

FIGURE 5.4 ● Pie Chart for Marital Status (marstat) With the Categories for Never Married and Married Individuals Only

Note: This pie chart is not proportional since the categories are not exhaustive.

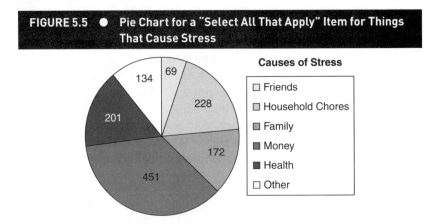

FIGURE 5.5 ● Pie Chart for a "Select All That Apply" Item for Things That Cause Stress

intuitive presentation of data. This type of "check all that apply" data would need a more complex design to represent the overlapping categories visually.

Presentation and Interpretation Issues

Pie charts do not have a scale on the *y*-axis like bar graphs because they are showing the relative contribution of a single section to the whole pie. For example, Figure 5.6 illustrates the relative frequencies for self-rated satisfaction with overall health (healthsatis) in a pie chart. This pie chart should be interpreted in the following way (see Figure 5.7). Therefore, if an individual is interested in comparing the size of one category relative to another category, it is more appropriate to use a bar chart (Figures 5.8 and 5.9).

When a pie chart is necessary (which is rare), you should include relative percentages or proportions within individual sections in order to help parse

FIGURE 5.6 ● Pie Chart for Health Satisfaction (healthsatis)

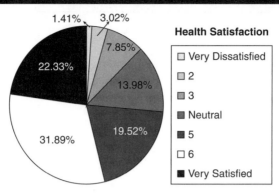

FIGURE 5.7 ● Relative Contribution of Each Individual Slice

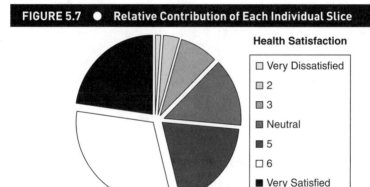

out details about the different relative contributions of an individual section. For example, in Figure 5.6, it would be difficult to ascertain the differential contribution of those who reported *neutral* (4) and *somewhat satisfied* (5) given the similarity in the overall area of each section. Another problem with the example is that there are too many categories, which leads to smaller slices and a more laborious interpretation. Since each individual section of a pie chart must be examined independently in order to assess its contribution to the full proportion, interpretation becomes an overwhelming and complex task if there are too many categories. For these reasons, many individuals caution against using pie charts in favor of bar graphs.

Bar graphs are useful for presenting absolute frequencies and percentages, and pie charts can be useful for illustrating relative frequencies and percentages. However, the cumulative properties of each category are not presented in either of these types of data visualization. In order to illustrate the *cumulative* nature of data for a variable, researchers use cumulative frequency polygons.

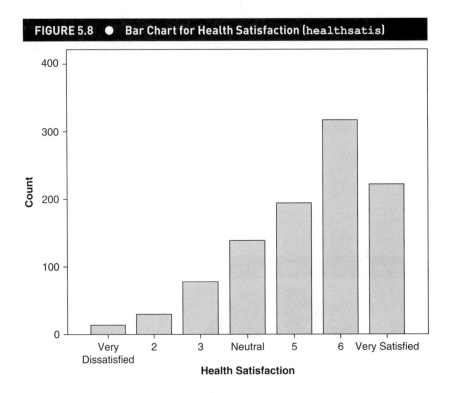

FIGURE 5.8 ● Bar Chart for Health Satisfaction (`healthsatis`)

Cumulative Frequency Polygons

Cumulative frequency polygons chart frequencies across multiple categories, except they also include *all preceding frequencies* (a running total). Therefore, cumulative frequency polygons are useful for graphing ordinal-level variables or grouped frequencies for interval/ratio variables. The cumulative percent is represented along the *y*-axis and trends upward to 100% as it approaches the highest category. The curvature reflects the gradual cumulative increase. Once the graph reaches the rightmost (highest) category, all individuals are represented (otherwise known as saturation). This graph therefore allows for interpretation of percentiles and quartiles, including the median.

Figure 5.9 presents a cumulative frequency polygon for individuals' self-rated level of overall stress (`stress`) for our nonrandom sample of 1,000 U.S. adults. The measure of stress is on a seven-point scale with 1 indicating that a person reported being *not at all stressed* and 7 indicating that he or she is *extremely stressed*. Each of the ordered categories for overall stress is represented along the *x*-axis. The *y*-axis illustrates the cumulative total for individuals in that category and all preceding categories. A guideline for interpreting the quartiles of the distribution in a cumulative frequency polygon is to find the percentile on the *y*-axis and trace it to the area of the line that falls in

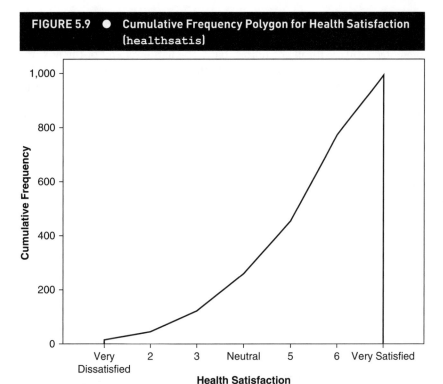

FIGURE 5.9 ● Cumulative Frequency Polygon for Health Satisfaction (healthsatis)

that percentile. For example, the graph in Figure 5.9 indicates that the 50th percentile—the median—is (3) *somewhat stressed*.

Presentation and Interpretation Issues

The interpretation of cumulative frequency polygons is pretty straightforward. However, it is important to confirm that the *y*-axis adds up to 100% on a cumulative frequency plot. Additionally, if cumulative frequencies and cumulative percentages are presented on opposite sides of the graph (which would facilitate interpretation), then the scale markers for the cumulative percent should align precisely with the corresponding cumulative *N*.

Boxplots

Boxplots, also known as box-and-whisker plots, are useful visual tools to present measures of central tendency and variability discussed in Chapter 6. As such, these graphs provide useful illustrations of the important characteristics of the distribution (i.e., distribution shape, central tendency, variability, and outliers) of interval/ratio data. There are a number of features that help a researcher interpret the distribution of a given variable.

Boxplots can be presented on the horizontal (*x*) or vertical (*y*) axis, but the interpretation is the same. The boxplot consists of a box (rectangle) that can be presented either vertically or horizontally. The left/lower end of the box, the **lower bound**, marks the first quartile of the variable's distribution. The right/upper end of the box, or the **upper bound**, indicates where the third quartile of the distribution lies. Therefore, the box itself represents the middle range of the data, with the median marked by a line. The **whiskers** are the areas that represent the range of data on either side of the quartile distribution, with end markers for the lowest and highest values.

With all of this information, you can interpret a number of features about the distribution based on four pieces of information: the range from the lowest to the highest observation, the median, and the upper and lower quartiles.

When interpreting, the distribution is symmetrical if (a) the line representing the median is in the middle of the box and (b) the whiskers are the same size. However, a distribution is skewed if the median is closer to one side or if one whisker is longer than the other. Figure 5.10 presents a boxplot for the variable age. In this example, there appears to be a fair amount of variability in the data given that the upper and lower hinges are far apart from each other. The box is approximately central in the distribution and the median is located in the middle of the box, which suggests that the distribution is approximately normal.

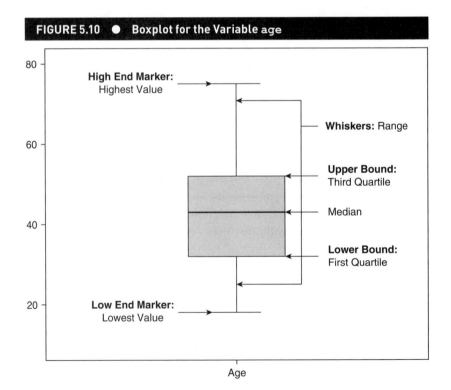

FIGURE 5.10 ● Boxplot for the Variable age

Age

Presentation and Interpretation Issues

Additional information is often needed to identify if outliers reflect the minimum and maximum values. This information can usually be added in the boxplot options of standard statistical software packages. In particular, a **modified boxplot** signals outliers in the extremes of the distribution; they are represented outside of the pattern of the data with symbols. For example, Figure 5.11 presents a modified boxplot for data on `weight` among U.S. adults ($N = 1,000$). Given that the median is approximately centered inside the box, this is an indication that there is a somewhat symmetrical distribution (because the middle of the data is centered between the first and third quartiles). However, several additional factors suggest that the data have a non-normal distribution. First, the median is not located between the highest and lowest values in the data—it is in the lower half. Second, the top whisker is longer than the bottom whisker, which means there is more variability in higher weight ranges. Third, there are several mild outliers in the upper bounds of the data, represented by circles—and an extreme outlier beyond the upper hinge, which is flagged with a star. At the same time, there is only a single mild outlier in the lower half. As such, the boxplot suggests that the data for `weight` are positively skewed.

FIGURE 5.11 ● Boxplot for the Variable `weight`

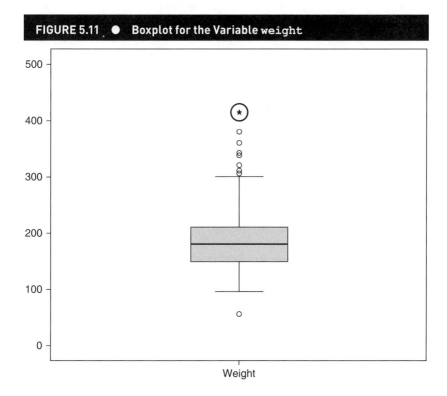

Weight

Stem and Leaf Plots

Stem and leaf plots are a way of presenting a large group of numbers in categories based on their units. It is essentially a way of both organizing data and presenting it visually. In a stem and leaf plot, the values are presented from the lowest to the highest score and are separated into two parts: the stem and the leaves. The **stem** represents the first digit or digits of the number, which are usually displayed on the left side of the plot. The **leaves** are commonly presented to the right of the stem and consist of the last digit or digits that correspond to the beginning digits represented by the stem. The **plot legend** describes how to transform the stem in order to interpret the data.

There are several things to observe when interpreting a stem and leaf plot. First, identify peaks in the plot, which represent high frequencies associated with those stems. Second, assess the variation in values (both within and across the stems) in order to identify (a) areas with missing values and (b) the symmetry of the distribution. Third, identify outliers that are present in the lower and upper extremes.

Figure 5.12 presents a stem and leaf plot for age on a small subset of men and women ($n = 25$). As part of the table description, the stem is identified as being reduced in the tens. Therefore, the second digit was left off the stem values, so each value must be multiplied by 10 when being interpreted. On the other hand, if the stem was reduced by hundreds (stem width = 100), then the stem would need to be multiplied by 100 for interpretation. Depending on the number of values in the data, the same stems might be reported on multiple lines with a cutoff point that drops to the next line. In this example, each stem

---

FIGURE 5.12 ● Stem and Leaf Plot for age for 25 Randomly Selected Cases

```
age Stem-and-Leaf Plot

 Frequency     Stem &  Leaf

      .00        2 .
     2.00        2 .  56
     5.00        3 .  00234
     3.00        3 .  788
     1.00        4 .  2
     4.00        4 .  5788
     4.00        5 .  0112
     3.00        5 .  689
     2.00        6 .  02
     1.00        6 .  6

 Stem width:    10
 Each leaf:        1 case(s)
```

occupies two lines to accommodate multiple leaf values. For each stem value, the leaves with low digits (0, 1, 2, 3, and 4) correspond to the first—top—part of the stem value, and those with higher digits (5, 6, 7, 8, and 9) correspond to the second—bottom—part of the stem value.

The first stem "2" represents the number 20, and since there are two stems for each series of numbers, the top stem identifies individuals in their early 20s. Since there are no leaves within this stem, there are no individuals in their early 20s in this subsample. The lower stem for "2" represents the late 20s. The leaves indicate that there are two individuals in their late 20s in the subsample—one who is 25 and another who is 26. There are five leaves corresponding to the top stem value for "3" (early 30s), which is the most populated age category in the subsample. The two zeroes in the leaves indicate that two individuals are 30 years old, followed by one individual each reporting 32, 33, and 34. Skipping to the highest age represented in the sample, there is a single individual at 66 years old. Altogether, the stem and leaf plot is an intuitive and concise breakdown of the actual values in the data. It allows a researcher to identify the minimum and maximum values, the range and variability, and where values tend to cluster.

Presentation and Interpretation Issues

One strength of stem and leaf plots is that they retain the actual scores in the data, whereas other methods collapse data into visual graphics or frequency table categories. However, the plots are difficult to interpret if (a) the scores for a given variable include decimal points and/or (b) the sample size is large. Consider the data on the full sample, presented in Figure 5.13. It would be difficult to ascertain information on frequencies based on this information given the size of the full data set. Again, the plot is divided into two parts: the stem and the leaf. The outliers are identified on either end of the stem and leaf plot—one case reported a weight of ≤55, and 11 cases are ≥305. These extremes are consistent with the values for `weight` in the boxplot example presented in the previous section.

Based on the description of the plot, the stem must be multiplied by 10 similar to the previous example. However, because of the large sample size, each leaf value now represents *two* cases—and an ampersand indicates that other values are present but did not meet the "two cases" rule. For example, the first stem is 9 and is followed by a leaf value of 6. This indicates that two individuals reported a weight of 96 pounds. The ampersand means that some other weight value in the 90s was also present, but since there were not two cases for the value, it was neither identified nor specified among the leaves. As a result, interpretation of stem and leaf plots for large samples is often onerous. In most cases, histograms (Chapter 4) are a more appropriate tool for examining the distribution of interval/ratio variables in data with large samples.

FIGURE 5.13 ● Full Stem and Leaf Plot for the Variable weight

```
weight Stem-and-Leaf Plot

Frequency     Stem &  Leaf

     1.00 Extremes    (= <55)
     4.00       9 .  6&
    10.00      10 .  0357&
    43.00      11 .  00000002255567888899&
    45.00      12 .  00003555555555667789&
    81.00      13 .  00000000000022244555555555556667778888&
    67.00      14 .  00000000000022334555555555555578&
    70.00      15 .  0000000000000000000255555555567788&
    89.00      16 .  00000000000022224445555555555555555555556
                     8899&
    87.00      17 .  00000000000000000003455555555555555555678
                     889&
   101.00      18 .  00000000000000000000022335555555555555555
                     5555788&&
    78.00      19 .  00000000000000000000001235555555556788
    74.00      20 .  00000000000000000000000000000025555589
    56.00      21 .  000000000000000345555555557&
    62.00      22 .  00000000000000004455555555555&
    32.00      23 .  000000000025555&
    30.00      24 .  00000000000555&
    20.00      25 .  0000000005
    14.00      26 .  00555&
     7.00      27 .  005&
    10.00      28 .  0005&
     2.00      29 .  &
     6.00      30 .  000
    11.00 Extremes    (> = 305)

Stem width:    10
Each leaf:       2 case(s)

& denotes fractional leaves.
```

Bivariate Data Visualization

Visualization techniques can also be used to provide visual cues about the relationship between two or more variables. Some of these techniques require the
presentation of charts and graphs mentioned earlier (e.g., boxplot, stem and
leaf plot) for multiple groups for comparison. For example, in order to compare
income distributions between men and women, a researcher might present
separate boxplots for men and women. Doing so would allow for examination of the income range, median, and upper and lower quartiles for men and

women separately. This section discusses a number of commonly used bivariate data visualizations: clustered and stacked bar graphs, line graphs, and scatterplots. Within each section, additional types of visualization for multivariate visualization are discussed; however, this chapter does not cover those types of charts and graphs in detail.

Clustered Bar Graphs

Clustered bar graphs, also known as grouped bar graphs or charts, are a common way of visually presenting a relationship between two categorical (nominal, ordinal, or dichotomous) variables. **Clustered bar graphs** visually present the breakdown of one variable across different categories of another variable. In other words, these charts are data visualizations of the information found in contingency tables, discussed in Chapter 4. For example, Figure 5.14 presents a clustered bar graph for the relationship between sex and job satisfaction (jobsatis), which has three categories: *dissatisfied* (1), *neutral* (2), and *satisfied* (3). This clustered bar graph is a visual presentation of the values in Table 5.2.

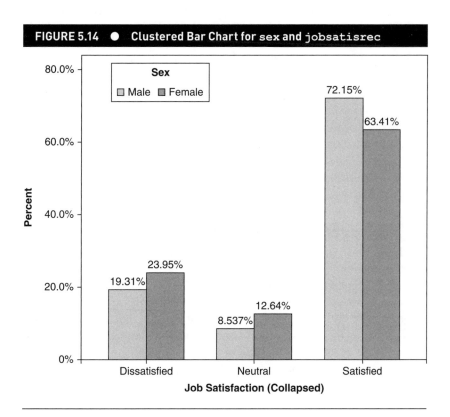

FIGURE 5.14 ● Clustered Bar Chart for sex and jobsatisrec

Note: Data labels are for comparison with the values in Table 5.2.

TABLE 5.2 ● Contingency Table With sex as the Column Variable and Job Satisfaction (jobsatis) as the Row Variable					
jobsatis*sex Contingency Table					
			Sex		
			Male	Female	Total
Job satisfaction	Dissatisfied	Count	95	108	203
		% within sex	19.3%	23.9%	21.5%
	Neutral	Count	42	57	99
		% within sex	8.5%	12.6%	10.5%
	Satisfied	Count	355	286	641
		% within sex	72.2%	63.4%	68.0%
Total		Count	492	451	943
		% within sex	100.0%	100.0%	100.0%

In Figure 5.14, there appear to be some minor differences between men and women with regard to their job satisfaction. In particular, men are more likely than women to report feeling satisfied with their job, and women are slightly more likely than men to report feeling neutral or dissatisfied with their job. The clustered bar chart is marked with data counts to help you map the values in the graph onto the values in the contingency table. Of those who responded that they were satisfied with their job, 38% were men, and 30% were women. Among those who reported feeling neutral about their job, 6% were women, and about 5% were men. Of the individuals who reported feeling dissatisfied, 10% were men and almost 12% were women. This graph allows for quick comparison between men and women on the jobsatis variable because the bars for job satisfaction are "clustered" together for men and women separately.

Presentation and Interpretation Issues

Clustered bar graphs are useful for presenting the breakdown of a variable across categories of another. However, when there are many categories on one variable, interpretation might become difficult. For example, Figure 5.15 presents a bar graph for sex and self-rated physical attractiveness (srattract), which ranges from 1 to 10. This is a complex graph that would be difficult to read. Rather than presenting this breakdown as a grouped bar chart, another option would be to present this as a stacked bar graph, which is discussed in the next section.

Bivariate bar graphs have also been used to present measures of central tendency for interval/ratio variables across different categories of a nominal variable. However, outliers might be masked in these graphs, which can lead to misinterpretation of the differences between groups. For example, a bar chart illustrating the mean weight for women and men separately might be

FIGURE 5.15   ●   Clustered Bar Graph for sex and srattract

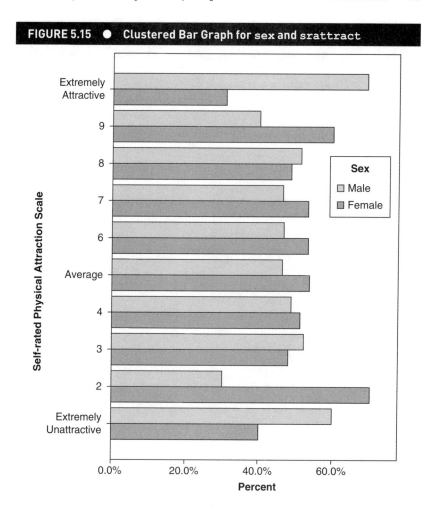

influenced by an outlier or outliers for either group. As such, instead of using a clustered bar graph, a more appropriate data visualization would be to explore separate modified boxplots for men and women, which would point to differences in the distribution and identify any outliers.

Stacked Bar Graphs

Another way of presenting the breakdown of a variable across the categories of another is through the use of a **stacked bar chart**, which combines multiple bars (variable categories) into a single column for each category of the independent variable. Stacked bar graphs can be presented to illustrate frequencies and relative percentages.

Figure 5.16 presents a **stacked bar graph** for two of the variables discussed earlier, sex and jobsatis. Instead of a side-by-side presentation, the

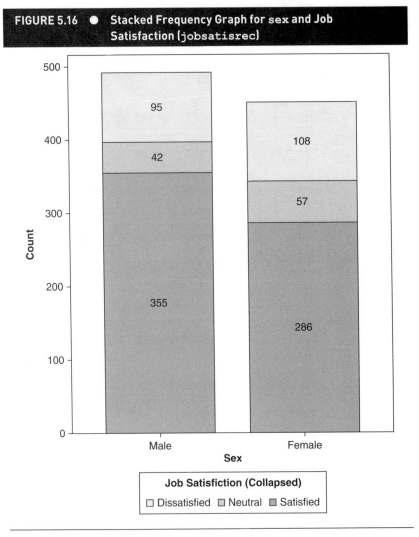

FIGURE 5.16 ● Stacked Frequency Graph for sex and Job Satisfaction (jobsatisrec)

Note: Data values are included for comparison with Table 5.2.

categories for *dissatisfied* (1), *neutral* (2), and *satisfied* (3) are collapsed into a single column. The legend helps identify which stacked section represents the frequencies for each job satisfaction category. The information in Figure 5.16 can be mapped back onto the values presented in Table 5.2.

Another way of presenting the data is to examine a stacked graph that provides relative frequencies separately for different groups (Figure 5.17). In this example, the categories are presented as relative frequencies (parts of a whole) for each category. In this graph, the breakdown of each job satisfaction category is presented separately with categories presented in their contribution

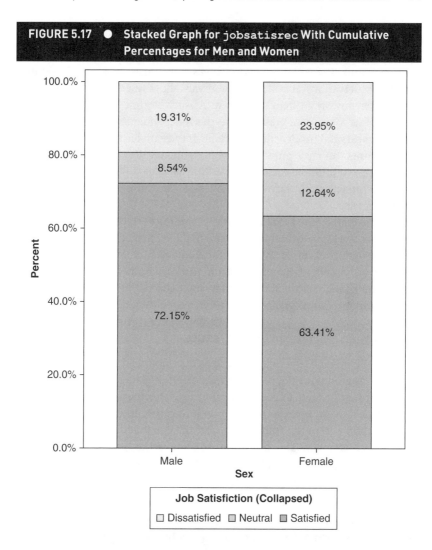

FIGURE 5.17 ● **Stacked Graph for `jobsatisrec` With Cumulative Percentages for Men and Women**

to 100% of the women and 100% of the men. This is basically the equivalent to presenting individual pie charts for men and women.

Presentation and Interpretation Issues

With many categories, interpretation of a stacked bar chart becomes difficult because the uppermost categories for job satisfaction do not share a common baseline on the *x*-axis the way the bottom categories do. As such, it is more difficult to compare between men and women across these categories. When interpretation of a stacked bar graph is difficult, a side-by-side visual (i.e., a clustered bar graph) might work better.

Time Series Graphs

Time series graphs are a type of line graph (and are sometimes referred to as a line graph). These graphs chart changes over consistent intervals of time. Repeated observations at consistent intervals allow researchers to track patterns and trends on an item of interest. As such, a time series graph can be thought of as a bivariate graph where the independent variable is the time itself (e.g., year) and the dependent variable is the variable that is observed over time. The lines can represent (a) change in frequency of one variable over time or (b) change in multiple categories over time. The data points in a line graph can also represent an average—or the average with minimum and maximum values over time.

Since the lines on the y-axis are plotted according to the time intervals on the x-axis (days, weeks, months, quarters, years), there must be consistent intervals on the x-axis. For example, Figure 5.18 presents a time series graph showing how rates of household mobility (moving to a new home) have changed over time in the United States. Since the data are collected by the Census Bureau each year, trends can be graphed over time.

Presentation and Interpretation Issues

Unlike a bar graph, the time series chart does not need to start at a baseline zero since (a) groups are not being compared and (b) data points do not always start at zero. For example, people always move—so the x-axis in Figure 5.18 does not need to be interpreted based on a zero baseline. However, zooming in on a certain area of the graph can distort the graph and its interpretation.

One problem with the distortion of time series graphs is **distorted scaling**—manipulating a graph's scale. In this case, one way to distort the scale of a time series graph is to use inconsistent time intervals. In the following time

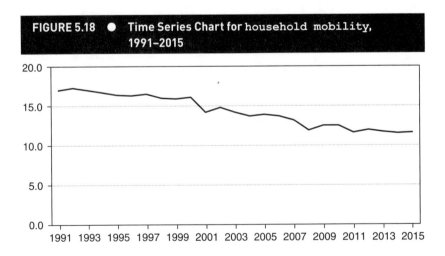

FIGURE 5.18 ● **Time Series Chart for household mobility, 1991–2015**

series plot (Figure 5.19), it appears as though the rate is changing over time; however, note that the scores on the x-axis are neither incremental nor consistent. At first, there is a single-unit increase in years; however, after 5 years, the intervals become larger. The distortion in presentation of these data exaggerates the downward trend shown in Figure 5.18.

Scatterplots

Up to this point, the y-axis has been used to represent *frequencies* in graphs. However, the y-axis can also represent an individual number when the variables are interval/ratio-level variables. Therefore, the assigned designation for the independent and dependent variables is important for interpretation. The general convention is that the independent variable is presented along the x-axis and the dependent variable is presented along the y-axis.

Scatterplots present the relationship between two interval/ratio variables.[2] The data are encoded, or plotted, simultaneously on the x-axis (IV) and y-axis (DV) in order to indicate how two variables are related. They are read left to right, with the y-axis markers on the left-hand side. For scatterplots, coordinates are plotted based on the value of both of the variables. The x-axis plots a specific number and the y-axis plots the other—thus allowing for a single plotted dot on a Cartesian plane. Since data points in quantitative variables can be negative, the axis does not always need to start at zero for a scatterplot.

Individuals who are plotted in the upper right quadrant of the plane scored high on the independent variable (x-axis) and high on the dependent variable (y-axis). A plotted dot in the lower right quadrant is an individual who had a high score on the x-axis and a low score on the y-axis. If one were to draw a line

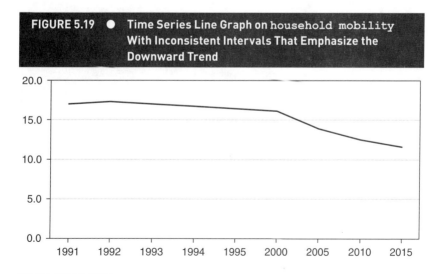

FIGURE 5.19 ● Time Series Line Graph on household mobility With Inconsistent Intervals That Emphasize the Downward Trend

[2] Scatterplots are also known as scattergrams, scatter diagrams, and Cartesian graphs.

from each plotted value, the scatterplot becomes a **line graph**, which plots change across each value on the y-axis (similar to the time series plot without the consistent temporal order plotted on the x-axis).

Figure 5.20 presents a scatterplot with values on the coordinates plotted for `weight` and height in inches (`height`) for the 15 individuals in Table 5.3. Each individual's pair of scores is represented by a single point on the scatterplot. For example, Respondent 3 (`idnum`) reported a weight of 217 pounds (which is located along the y-axis) and 73 inches in height (located along the x-axis). Therefore, the pair of scores for this individual are coordinates for the plot. The score on the x-axis is the first value in the coordinate, followed by the score on the y-axis: (73, 217). The location where those coordinates match is in the upper right quadrant of the graph, which corresponds to a high score on height and a high score on weight.

Respondent 6 (`idnum`) reported a weight of 112 pounds—which is low on the y-axis—and a height of 63 inches—which is low on the x-axis. Therefore, the individual is plotted along the coordinates (63, 112), which is located in the bottom left quadrant of the graph, indicating a low score on both height

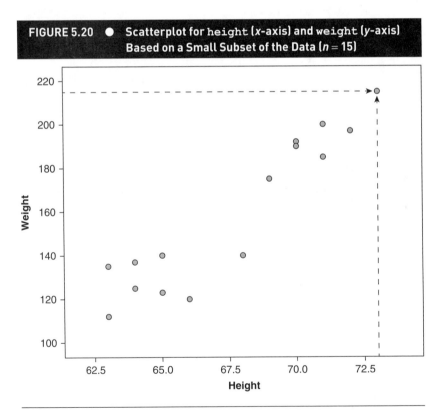

FIGURE 5.20 ● Scatterplot for `height` (x-axis) and `weight` (y-axis) Based on a Small Subset of the Data (n = 15)

Note: The dashed lines point to the plot on the coordinates (73, 217).

TABLE 5.3 ● ID Numbers and Data for a Small Subsample of 15 Individuals' height in Inches and weight		
Id	Height	weight
651	65	123
666	63	135
693	73	215
730	65	140
737	64	125
750	63	112
796	71	185
830	71	200
900	64	137
916	69	175
990	66	120
996	70	192
1001	70	190
1049	68	140
1121	72	197

and weight. Therefore, the trend between height and weight is linear and positive, with higher scores on weight corresponding to higher scores on height. This is an example of a positive correlation, which was discussed in Chapter 2. Higher scores on weight are associated with higher scores on height—and, conversely, lower scores on weight correspond to lower scores on height. This is represented with a line on the scatterplot in Figure 5.20 that moves from the lower left to the upper right.

An example of a negative correlation is presented in Figure 5.21, which presents data on the age at which an individual's first child was born (agefirstbirth) and that individual's number of children (kidnum) for 15 individuals. In this scatterplot, the plotted points move from the upper left quadrant to the lower right quadrant, indicating that there is a negative relationship between the two variables. In other words, in this small sample, those who have their first child at a young age appear to have a higher number of children. Those who have their first child at older ages tend to have a smaller total number of children. Additionally, a dashed line is included to represent the mean total number of children. This allows for faster processing of who lies above versus below the mean score based on where their score is on the x-axis.

The direction of a bivariate relationship and the magnitude of the correlation between two interval/ratio variables is conveyed numerically in the form

FIGURE 5.21 ● **Scatterplot Between Age First Kid Was Born (`agefirstbirth`) and Total Number of Children (`kidnum`) Using a Small Subset of the Data (*n* = 15)**

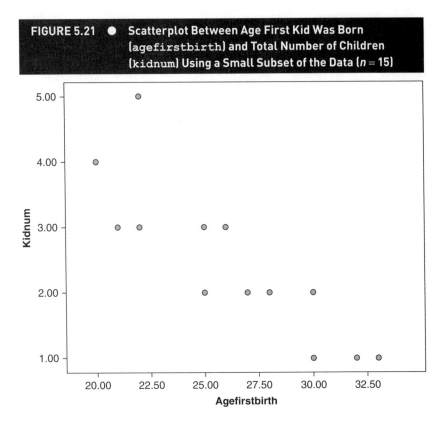

of a correlation coefficient, which is discussed further in Chapter 11. However, not all relationships between interval/ratio variables are **linear**, which means they form an approximate line. Researchers often encounter other types of relationships in the data, such as curvilinear shapes and accelerated change.

Presentation and Interpretation Issues

Scatterplots are especially difficult to interpret when a sample is large and the values are clustered around the same coordinates. This can be seen in Figure 5.22, which plots coordinates for `height` and `weight` for the full sample of 1,000 individuals. The same approximately linear trend is somewhat apparent (e.g., low scores on height correspond to low scores on weight), but the presentation is less intuitive than the scatterplot with the smaller sample discussed earlier.

When interpreting data on a scatterplot, make sure the intervals are consistent. As with time series graphs, the interpretation changes based on the scale—and an inconsistent scale on either axis can lead to a distorted interpretation of the relationship between the two variables.

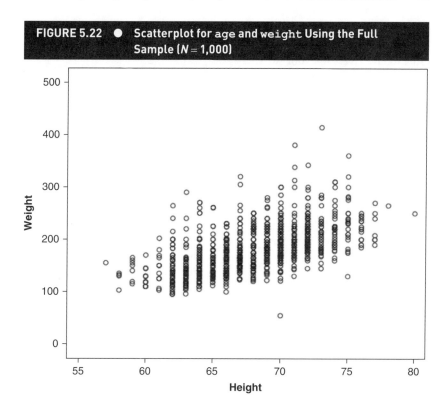

FIGURE 5.22 ● Scatterplot for age and weight Using the Full Sample (*N* = 1,000)

Visual Presentation

A final point on the presentation of visualization is necessary. In order to effectively interpret charts and graphs, researchers must understand that interpretation is largely influenced by the way the data are presented. For example, cluttered graphs with too many colors might unnecessarily complicate the information being presented; once a visualization is chosen, consider carefully whether the same story can be told with fewer adornments. If so, it might ease interpretation to keep extraneous information to a minimum. For example, it is generally frowned upon to present univariate and bivariate data in 3D charts because, while they do add to the visual appeal, they can lead to the distortion of data (especially when the charts are tilted). Therefore, many suggest avoiding the practice altogether.

Conclusion

The art of presenting data visually is essentially using statistics and creativity to quickly communicate a story that exists in your data. The purpose of this chapter was to help you present and interpret data visualizations more effectively.

When a data visualization is inefficient and unintuitive, additional footwork is necessary to make sense of a chart. This extra work should be minimized in order to effectively tell your story.

Terms

bar graphs 60
boxplots 67
clustered bar graphs 73
cumulative frequency
   polygons 66
distorted scaling 78
leaves 70
line graph 80
linear 82
lower bound 68
modified boxplot 69

pie chart 63
plot legend 70
scatterplots 79
stacked bar chart 75
stacked bar
   graph 75
stem 70
stem and leaf plots 70
truncated graph 61
upper bound 68
whiskers 68

Central Tendency and Variability

Understanding How to Calculate and Interpret Measures of Central Tendency

What Is a Measure of Central Tendency?

A measure of central tendency is a number that tells you what is average or typical in a distribution. Another way to think about it is that a measure of central tendency illustrates where the middle of a distribution lies.

Of course, how you go about choosing and calculating measures of central tendency depends upon the variable that you are analyzing. The way you approach the variable "respondent's favorite color" will be different from the way you approach "respondent's annual income." The key difference lies in the level of measurement for each variable.

As explained in Chapter 2, variables can be considered as either nominal, ordinal, interval, or ratio. Because some types of variables contain more information than others, there is a sort of hierarchy of information that offers greater flexibility for some variables over others (depending upon how much information is measured within the variable in its current state). Keep in mind that there is more than just one way to measure a variable. Consider students' grades in a particular class. Is there only one way to have knowledge of students' performance? Of course not—there are many ways. For example, you might have the percent score for each student. Also, you might just have the letter grade recorded in a file. For some purposes, you may only need to know whether the student passed or failed the class. These three ways to measure class performance all contain different amounts of information, and all have a different purpose (e.g., letter grade information is needed for college/university transcripts).

The **cumulative property of levels of measurement** provides that variables measured at higher levels can be treated as if they were measured at lower levels. The reason for this is that for the variables at higher levels, you can "give up" some information to transform the variable to a lower level of measurement (see Figure 6.1 for a quick diagram). Notice, too, that a dichotomous variable is an exception in that those variables can be treated as either nominal, ordinal, interval, or ratio, since there are only two categories and therefore do not have an order that can be disrupted; furthermore, discrete variables comply in this case since the outcomes provided do not necessarily need to be discrete for these measures. As an example, think about the number of children in each respondent's family. Clearly, this is a discrete variable since one family cannot have half or some other fraction of a child. Children cannot literally be divided, cut in half, and so on. (Doing so would be a terrible crime!) However, as you will see, the average number of children in families in a particular city might be 2.5; this average is computed without slicing any children in half!

Variables Measured at the Nominal Level

For nominal variables, you will remember (Chapter 2) that categories varying by like or kind, but without a mathematical interpretation, are measured at the nominal level.

Here are a few more examples of nominally measured variables:

- Respondent's favorite color
  - blue, red, green, purple, pink, orange, and so on

FIGURE 6.1 ● Cumulative Property of Levels of Measurement

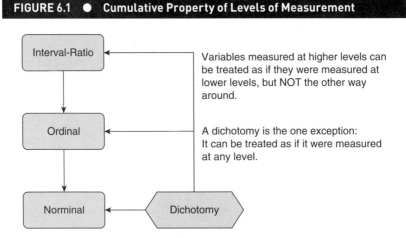

Interval-Ratio

Ordinal

Norminal   Dichotomy

Variables measured at higher levels can be treated as if they were measured at lower levels, but NOT the other way around.

A dichotomy is the one exception: It can be treated as if it were measured at any level.

- Respondent's religious affiliation

  ○ Methodist, Presbyterian, Lutheran, Baptist, Catholic, Jewish, Muslim, Unitarian Universalist, Church of Christ, none, and so on

  ○ As you know, there are other ways to measure "religiosity" that not only vary in level of measurement from "religious affiliation," but also in the concept itself. One example of this would be "how often the respondent attends religious services." This is a separate variable, independent of respondent's religious affiliation. Depending on how much detail regarding the frequency of attendance is collected and categorized, this variable could be designed to be measured as interval-ratio, ordinal, or nominal level.

- Breed of dog
  ○ Australian Cattle Dog, Jack Russell Terrier, Labrador Retriever, Corgi, Beagle, Dachshund, Boxer, Chihuahua, German Shepherd, Maltese, Doberman, and so on. And do not forget about mixed-breed dogs, who could be categorized into one category, or by their primary breed, or by some other purposeful rubric.

So, how do you describe what might be average or typical of one of these distributions? Conceptualizing the "middle" of such a distribution might be difficult. Particularly for nominal variables with a relatively small number of categories (attributes), the mode serves as the appropriate measure of central tendency. In fact, it is the only measure of central tendency that may be used (unless the nominal variable happens to be a dichotomy, for reasons discussed earlier).

The **mode** represents the category or attribute with the largest frequency.

One way to think about the mode would be an election. Who wins? Generally, the candidate who represents the mode (having the highest frequency of votes) will win. (We will not go into the more complicated election details for some nonmajority situations that may result in runoffs, etc., in some jurisdictions.) In Figure 6.2, you will see that Mina, the dog, won the election in fictitious Minasberg by receiving more votes than the other two candidates. I wonder how she scored such a landslide victory—perhaps it's because she supports single-payer treats for all residents of Minasberg!

If two categories have the highest (same) frequency, then the distribution is said to be bimodal. Of course, if there is more than one mode, the distribution is multimodal (bimodal, trimodal, etc.).

So if, at the local animal shelter, you find 20 Chihuahuas, 3 Dachshunds, 1 Beagle, 20 Pit Bulls, and 2 Australian Cattle Dogs, this hypothetical distribution would be bimodal: the modes are Pit Bull and Chihuahua (20 dogs in each category).

FIGURE 6.2 ● Poll Result for Minasberg Mayoral Election

| 23,567 | 95,754 | 22,449 |

141,770 total votes cast

Image of Clinton: Wikimedia Commons. *Image of Mina:* photo by Billy Wagner. *Image of Trump:* Wikimedia Commons.

Variables Measured at the Ordinal Level

Since variables measured at the ordinal level have order or rank, it is often advantageous to use a measure of central tendency that incorporates this information. The **median** is the case or respondent in the distribution below which 50% of the distribution falls. Therefore, the median is truly the *middle* score.

Have you ever driven on a road where there happens to be something called a median strip? It should be no surprise that about half of the road is on one side and about half the road is on the other side; the median, or median strip, divides the road into two approximately equal halves. The same is true of the statistical median: It divides the distribution approximately in half.

What if there is no middle score, case, or respondent—what if there are an even number of scores in the distribution?

In that case, if the variable is continuous, you would take the average of the two middle scores (add both scores together and divide by 2). If the variable is nominal or ordinal and the two middle score categories are the same, this is easy—the median is that category. If, however, the two middle score categories are different, you would say that the median falls between Category A and Category B, where A and B represent the names of the categories.

Variables Measured at the Interval or Ratio Level

Variables measured at the interval-ratio level contain more information than other levels, so it would be beneficial to incorporate as much information as possible into a calculated measure. It is important to remember that there are times when it might benefit the research question to not use all of that information and invoke the cumulative property of levels of measurement. For now, however, let's focus on the interval-ratio level of measurement without making any of that kind of adjustment.

The **mean** is the arithmetic average of a distribution and an appropriate measure of central tendency for an interval-ratio distribution that is not skewed. For a more detailed explanation of a skewed distribution, see Chapter 4.

$$\bar{Y} = \frac{Y}{N}$$

where

Y = the value of each case

N = the total number of cases in the distribution

FIGURE 6.3 ● Odd Versus Even Number of Cases/Respondents

ODD: x x x x x X x x x x x   Use the middle score

EVEN: x x x x x X X x x x x x   Average the two middle scores

---

BOX 6.1

EXAMPLE 1

Suppose you are interested in knowing the average weight of dogs in a particular shelter. To compute the mean, you would add together all the weights of the dogs and divide by how many dogs there are. So, for instance . . .

32 lbs.	Dog 1
44 lbs.	Dog 2
9 lbs.	Dog 3
18 lbs.	Dog 4
29 lbs.	Dog 5
55 lbs.	Dog 6
80 lbs.	Dog 7
37 lbs.	Dog 8
25 lbs.	Dog 9
61 lbs.	Dog 10

Add the 10 weights together and then divide by 10 (since there are 10 dogs):

390 lbs. /10 dogs = 39 lbs. average weight (mean)

Often, scores on an interval-ratio variable might be grouped for easier consumption. If that is the case, the following formula may be used to calculate the mean:

$$\bar{Y} = \frac{fY}{N}$$

where
Y = the value of each case
N = the total number of cases in the distribution
f = the frequency of the group

If, however, the distribution is significantly skewed, the median will be a better measure of central tendency. This is because the median is the middle score and is not changed relatively more or less by scores that might be either particularly high or particularly low.

BOX 6.2
EXAMPLE 2

At another dog shelter, the following is a distribution that appears to be skewed. This shelter appears to house mostly very small dogs, but there also happens to be a very large dog present (perhaps a Saint Bernard or other large breed)! See how the mean is no longer a good representation of where the middle of the distribution lies?

9 lbs.	Dog 1
6 lbs.	Dog 2
8 lbs.	Dog 3
5 lbs.	Dog 4
9 lbs.	Dog 5
5 lbs.	Dog 6
7 lbs.	Dog 7
6 lbs.	Dog 8
8 lbs.	Dog 9
122 lbs.	Dog 10

Again, add the 10 weights together and then divide by 10 (since there are 10 dogs):

185 lbs./10 dogs = 18.5 lbs. average weight (mean)

In this case, what is computed for the average is more than double the size of all of the dogs in the distribution, except for the one dog who is much heavier than all the rest. As such, the mean does not provide a good representation of where the center of this distribution lies.

Instead, let's compute the median:

1. Put the dogs in order by their weights

5 lbs.	Dog 4
5 lbs.	Dog 6
6 lbs.	Dog 2
6 lbs.	Dog 8
7 lbs.	Dog 7
8 lbs.	Dog 3
8 lbs.	Dog 9
9 lbs.	Dog 1
9 lbs.	Dog 5
122 lbs.	Dog 10

2. Select the two middle cases

   Dog 7 and Dog 3 are in the middle of the distribution. Dog 7 weighs 7 lbs., and Dog 3 weighs 8 lbs.

3. Average those two weights

   The average of their two weights, (7 lbs. + 8 lbs.)/2, is equal to 7.5 lbs.

The median is equal to 7.5 lbs. As you can see from this example, the median better represents the distribution of elements in this case where there is a heavy positive skew.

When the distribution of an interval-ratio variable is significantly skewed, as it is in Example 2, the appropriate measure of central tendency to use would be the median. The median would provide the true middle score of the distribution (averaging the two middle scores if the distribution has an even number of elements).

Understanding How Individuals in a Distribution Vary Around a Central Tendency

Index of Qualitative Variation: Appropriateness, Calculation, Interpretation

The **index of qualitative variation (IQV)** is a measure of variability for nominal variables; it is the ratio of the total number of differences in the distribution to the maximum number of possible differences that could have theoretically occurred in that distribution. The formula that is used to calculate the IQV is as follows:

$$IQV = \frac{K(100^2 - \Sigma f^2)}{100^2(K - 1)}$$

where
K = the number of categories
N = the total number of cases in the distribution
Σf^2 = the sum of all squared frequencies or percentages

The result is a single number that expresses the diversity or dispersion of a (nominal/categorical) distribution. The minimum value of the IQV is 0 and the maximum is 1. If the IQV is equal to 0, then there is no diversity in the distribution; in other words, all elements are the same. If the IQV is equal to 1, then the distribution is maximally diverse; so, given the possible categories, the cases are spread out equally as much as possible (see Figure 6.4).

FIGURE 6.4 ●   The IQV: Extreme Values

Variable: Type of Shape

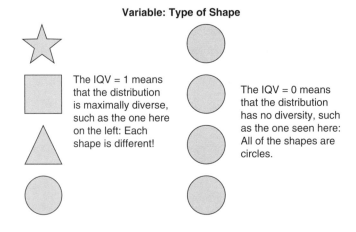

The IQV = 1 means that the distribution is maximally diverse, such as the one here on the left: Each shape is different!

The IQV = 0 means that the distribution has no diversity, such as the one seen here: All of the shapes are circles.

BOX 6.3

LEARNING CHECK: IQV AND DOG TOYS

The two images show Mina with three of her dog toys. In which of the images is the IQV for diversity of type of Mina's dog toys equal to 0, and in which image is it equal to 1?

Photo by Billy Wagner.

PHOTO 6.1 Scenario A: Mina is sitting next to three squirrel dog toys.

Photo by Billy Wagner.

PHOTO 6.2 Scenario B: Mina is sitting next to a squirrel and two different dog toys.

The answer to this learning check is at the end of this chapter (see page 96).

The IQV is useful in comparing the diversity or dispersion of distributions. Those distributions with higher IQVs have greater diversity than those with lower IQVs.

Range: Appropriateness, Calculation, Interpretation

The **range** is a measure of variation for interval-ratio variables. To compute the range, take the difference between the highest (maximum) and the lowest (minimum) scores in the distribution:

$$range = \text{maximum score} - \text{minimum score}$$

The greater the calculated range, the greater the dispersion within that distribution. While the range is very easy to calculate, it has a significant weakness as a measure of variability. If the distribution contains a single high or low outlier (or both), this can artificially inflate the perception of variability in a distribution. An **outlier** is a value that is significantly outside the interval of the rest of the scores in the distribution. If a distribution has an outlier or outliers, then the interquartile range will be a more appropriate measure of variability.

Interquartile Range: Appropriateness, Calculation, Interpretation

The **interquartile range (IQR)** is a measure of variation for interval-ratio variables. The IQR indicates the width of the middle 50% of a distribution. Because the IQR represents the middle half of the distribution, any outliers at either end of the distribution will not have an effect on the computed value of the IQR, making this a good measure of variability for distributions either with or without outliers. The IQR is defined as the difference between the lower and upper quartiles (Q1 and Q3). The lower quartile (Q1) represents the 25th percentile; the upper quartile (Q3) is marked by the 75th percentile.

$$IQR = Q3 - Q1$$

where
Q3 = 75th percentile
Q1 = 25th percentile

Variance: Appropriateness, Calculation, Interpretation

The **variance** is a measure of variation for interval-ratio variables. The variance is computed by taking the average of the squared deviations from the mean of the distribution:

$$s_Y^2 = \frac{\Sigma(Y - \bar{Y})^2}{N - 1}$$

where
$\bar{Y}$ = the distribution mean

The variance cannot be a negative number. This can be illustrated by examining the equation of the variance itself. The numerator is a value that will be squared, which necessarily results in a positive value. The denominator is a positive value (sample size) subtracting 1. The sample size cannot be a negative number and should not be a sample of size 1. Therefore, the denominator will be positive as well. Even if the sample size were equal to 1, in the extreme case, the variance would be zero (or undefined) and not equal to a negative number.

The possible values for the variance range from zero to infinity. Zero would indicate no variation whatsoever; all elements of the distribution would be the same on the variable being measured (e.g., all respondents having the exact same annual income would yield a variance of zero on the annual income variable). As the computed variance begins to increase, so too does the variation in the distribution.

Standard Deviation: Appropriateness, Calculation, Interpretation

The **standard deviation** is a measure of variation for interval-ratio variables. The standard deviation is calculated by taking the square root of the variance (see variance, discussed earlier):

$$s_Y = \sqrt{s_Y^2} = \sqrt{\frac{\Sigma(Y - \bar{Y})^2}{N - 1}}$$

where
$\bar{Y}$ = the distribution mean

Like the variance, the standard deviation cannot be negative. We know this must be the case since we have established that the variance cannot be negative. If the variance is positive and you take the square root of the variance, this will return a positive value. If, in an extreme case, the variance is equal to zero, then the square root of zero is zero.

Theoretically, the standard deviation can range from zero to infinity. At zero, the standard deviation would indicate that the distribution has absolutely no variation and therefore all elements of the distribution are the same on the dimension you are measuring (e.g., all members of your sample are exactly the same height in inches). While possible, this is not a common finding. As the calculated value of the standard deviation becomes larger, this is an indication of greater variation in the sample and, by extension (when using a representative sample), in the population.

The standard deviation is the most common measure of variability used for interval-ratio variables. It is particularly useful when utilizing knowledge from the standard normal distribution in an analysis, but also useful when comparing distributions to assess relative dispersion.

BOX 6.4
EXAMPLE 3

The mean weekly wage earned in Montgomery County, Maryland, during the second quarter of 2016 was $1,319 (Bureau of Labor Statistics, 2017). Suppose the standard deviation is $200. What does that tell us about the variation in weekly wages among workers in Montgomery County, Maryland?

Most important, the standard deviation is used as a measure to compare variation in one population to variation in another population. So, if we learn that in Howard County, Maryland, the average weekly wage was $1,197 per week (Bureau of Labor Statistics, 2017) and the standard deviation was $250, we would know that the variation in wages in Howard County is greater than in Montgomery County. The distribution of workers' weekly wages would be said to span a larger interval in the county with the greater standard deviation.

In Chapter 7, much greater detail is given to the role of standard deviation in terms of what it tells us about the population and how we can use it to calculate other things. For instance, if the mean is $1,319 and the standard deviation is $200, we know that roughly two-thirds of the distribution falls within one standard deviation of the mean. So, about two-thirds of the workers in Montgomery County, Maryland, can be estimated to earn between $1,119 and $1,519 per week.

Answer to Chapter 6 Learning Check

IQV = 0 (Scenario A); IQV = 1 (Scenario B)

Terms

cumulative property of levels of measurement 86
index of qualitative variation (IQV) 92
interquartile range (IQR) 94
mean 89

median 88
mode 87
outlier 94
range 94
standard deviation 95
variance 94

Reference

Bureau of Labor Statistics. (2017). *County employment and wages in Maryland— second quarter 2016*. Retrieved from https://www.bls.gov/regions/mid-atlantic/news-release/countyemploymentandwages_maryland.htm

What Are *z* Scores, and Why Are They Important?

What Is a *z* Score?

A **z score** or **standard score** is a value that denotes how many standard deviations away from the mean a particular raw score lies. This could be an indication of a raw score being either above or below the mean. A positive (+) z score is an indicator of a raw score that is greater than the mean. A negative (−) z score is an indicator of a raw score that is lower than the mean. As explained below, a z score that is neither positive nor negative, but equal to zero, is an indicator that the particular raw score happens to be equal to the value of the mean.

A raw score is the value of a particular case on a variable in your dataset. So, 65 inches might be the raw score for the variable `height` in your dataset. To compute the z score for that, we need some more information first.

Why Are *z* Scores Important?

In Chapter 4, the standard normal distribution was introduced. A great deal of information was provided about the normal distribution, and to be able to harness that knowledge to further analyze specific, real-world distributions is quite valuable. In order to use our knowledge about the standard normal distribution to make predictions about a population from a sample, we need to be able to see a particular score (respondent, case, etc.) as a standard score (z score) to determine where in the theoretical distribution that score lies.

Of course, it is important to remember that this work surrounding z scores ultimately involves using a sample to make predictions about a population using a theoretical family of distributions (the standard normal distribution). As such, it is assumed that the sample is representative of the population.

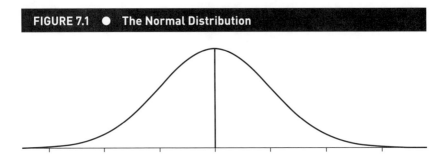

FIGURE 7.1 ● The Normal Distribution

You will remember that the normal distribution is a bell-shaped, symmetrical, theoretical distribution (see Figure 7.1). In fact, it is a family of theoretical distributions that adheres to certain principles. The mode, the median, and the mean are all equal, coinciding at the peak in the middle of this theoretical distribution. Frequencies decrease as you move in either direction toward the ends of the curve.

The normal distribution is an ideal distribution. Real-life empirical distributions will not perfectly mirror this ideal type. However, a great many things in life do approximate the normal distribution, and we can say that they are normally distributed. For more details about the normal distribution, review Chapter 4.

How to Calculate a *z* Score

Let's start with a real-world scenario and some data. In Dr. Wagner's biostatistics class, the mean score was 75/100 (75%) and the standard deviation of those scores was 10 percentage points.

We also know that the scores were approximately normally distributed. This information reveals a great deal: The middle of the distribution is at 75, and the standard deviation of 10 illustrates how steep the curve is on both sides. Moreover, we can use these two numbers in combination with the standard normal table to do great things!

BOX 7.1

QUICK LEARNING CHECK

What is the variance of the scores in Dr. Wagner's biostatistics course if the mean is 75/100 (75%) and the standard deviation of those scores is 10 percentage points?

The answer is at the end of this chapter.

To convert a raw score (your score earned in the class, for example), use the following formula:

$$z = \frac{Y - \bar{Y}}{s_y}$$

The z score, or standard score, represents how many standard deviations away from the mean that particular raw score lies. If the z score is positive, the raw (original) score is above the mean. If the z score is negative, the raw score is lower than the mean. If the z score is equal to zero, that means the raw score is equal to the mean (if your raw score is equal to the mean, there is no need to calculate; the z score is zero).

So, if your score is 80, we know the z score should be positive, since it is greater than the mean and therefore on the right side of the normal curve. To confirm:

$$z = (80 - 75)/10 = .5$$

So, the z score associated with a raw score of 80 in this distribution is .5 or ½. Indeed, this z score is positive. See Figure 7.2 for a visual representation.

What about a raw score of 60, someone who barely passed the course with a D–? It should be negative, since the raw score is less than the mean. To confirm:

$$z = (60 - 75)/10 = -1.5$$

So, the z score associated with a raw score of 60 in this distribution is –1.5, as shown in Figure 7.3.

Whenever you calculate a z score, it is always a good idea to make a quick check that the sign (positive or negative) of the z score makes sense. This is true whether starting with a raw score and converting to a z score as we just did, or whether starting with the z score and converting to a raw score.

How to Calculate a Raw Score From a *z* Score

Using the same data from earlier, where the mean score is 75 and the standard deviation is 10, how can we calculate the raw score? Through algebraic manipulation, the formula in the previous section can be transformed into this one:

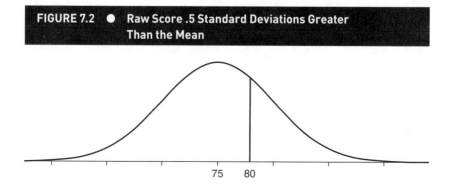

FIGURE 7.2 ●   Raw Score .5 Standard Deviations Greater Than the Mean

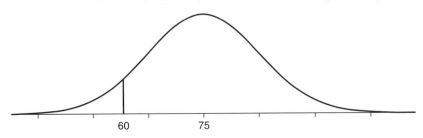

FIGURE 7.3 ● Raw Score 1.5 Standard Deviations Below the Mean

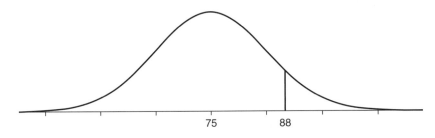

FIGURE 7.4 ● Standard Deviations Greater than the Mean

$$Y = z\left(s_y\right) + \bar{Y}$$

Suppose you are given the z score for your grade in the class, but want to know the raw (actual) score to which that corresponds. (This is a great tool for faculty to use in class: assign grades in z scores so that students will have to compute the raw score for practice!) Let's try this out: the z score for your grade is 1.3. Using the formula above, we get

$$Y = 1.3(10) + 75 = 88$$

So, the score is 88. Does this make sense? The z score is positive, indicating that the raw score must be higher than the mean. The raw score, 88, is greater than the mean, 75, so everything appears to be in order, as seen in Figure 7.4.

It is often quite helpful to make a quick sketch of a standard normal curve, placing the value of the mean in the middle. You can add other raw scores, as appropriate, above or below the mean. This is helpful for keeping track of where in the distribution values fall, and also for areas and probabilities (we are almost there; just a bit further into this chapter!).

The Standard Normal Table

Using a standard normal table or application to provide values is a way to determine probabilities associated with z scores and raw scores. Similarly, you can determine the z score and the raw score associated with a particular probability in a distribution. (See Table 7.1 for a partial listing of the standard normal table, and Appendix A for the full table.)

TABLE 7.1 ● The Standard Normal Table

The values in Column A are z scores. Column B lists the proportion of area between the mean and a given z. Column C lists the proportion of area beyond a given z. Only positive z scores are listed. Because the normal curve is symmetrical, the areas for negative z scores will be exactly the same as the areas for positive z scores.

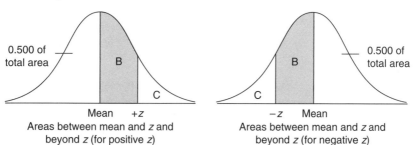

0.500 of total area — B — C — Mean +z
Areas between mean and z and beyond z (for positive z)

0.500 of total area — B — C — −z Mean
Areas between mean and z and beyond z (for negative z)

A	B	C
z	Area Between Mean and z	Area Beyond z
0.00	0.0000	0.5000
0.01	0.0040	0.4960
0.02	0.0080	0.4920
0.03	0.0120	0.4880
0.04	0.0160	0.4840
0.05	0.0199	0.4801
0.06	0.0239	0.4761
0.07	0.0279	0.4721
0.08	0.0319	0.4681
0.09	0.0359	0.4641
0.10	0.0398	0.4602
0.11	0.0438	0.4562
0.12	0.0478	0.4522
0.13	0.0517	0.4483
0.14	0.0557	0.4443
0.15	0.0596	0.4404
0.16	0.0636	0.4364
0.17	0.0675	0.4325

(Continued)

TABLE 7.1 ● (Continued)

A	B	C
z	Area Between Mean and z	Area Beyond z
0.18	0.0714	0.4286
0.19	0.0753	0.4247
0.20	0.0793	0.4207
0.21	0.0832	0.4168
0.22	0.0871	0.4129
0.23	0.0910	0.4090
0.24	0.0948	0.4052
0.25	0.0987	0.4013
0.26	0.1026	0.3974
0.27	0.1064	0.3936
0.28	0.1103	0.3897
0.29	0.1141	0.3859
0.30	0.1179	0.3821
0.31	0.1217	0.3783
0.32	0.1255	0.3745
0.33	0.1293	0.3707
0.34	0.1331	0.3669
0.35	0.1368	0.3632
0.36	0.1406	0.3594
0.37	0.1443	0.3557
0.38	0.1480	0.3520
0.39	0.1517	0.3483
0.40	0.1554	0.3446
0.41	0.1591	0.3409
0.42	0.1628	0.3372
0.43	0.1664	0.3336
0.44	0.1700	0.3300
0.45	0.1736	0.3264
0.46	0.1772	0.3228
0.47	0.1808	0.3192
0.48	0.1844	0.3156
0.49	0.1879	0.3121
0.50	0.1915	0.3085

Source: Frankfort-Nachmias, C., & Leon-Guerrero, A. (2017). *Social statistics for a diverse society* (8th ed.). Thousand Oaks, CA: Sage.

Areas Under the Curve (Probabilities)

Continuing with the earlier data, where the mean is equal to 75 and the standard deviation is equal to 10, we will demonstrate how to use the standard normal distribution (table) as a tool to answer many questions. To start, remember that when we are looking for probability, this is equivalent to the area under the standard normal curve. So, there is 100% of the area under the curve (proportion = 1.00), indicating that there is a 100% chance that your score falls somewhere in the universe of scores. Maximum and total probability is equal to 1; area under the curve is always equal to 1, as well. Of course, that obvious piece of information is not very helpful by itself. We can use the properties of the normal distribution to reveal more specific information that will be very useful in determining probabilities, ranges, and cut points.

1. What is the probability of falling into the interval between a particular raw score and the mean?

    What if that score is lower than the mean? Let's find the proportion/percentage of students whose scores are between 65 and 75 (see Figure 7.5).

    a. Convert 65 to a z score: $(65 - 75)/10 = -1$

    b. Remember that the normal distribution is symmetrical and that there is no such thing as negative area, so look for 1.00 in column A of the table, then move over to column C and here is what you should see: .3413. This reveals the area between 65 and 75 (the mean). Area is equal to probability. The proportion can be converted to a percentage: .3413 = 34.13%.

    This is also a good time to reflect: If 34.13% of the area/probability falls between one standard deviation and the mean on the left side of

FIGURE 7.5 ● Probability (Area) Between the Mean and a Score Below the Mean

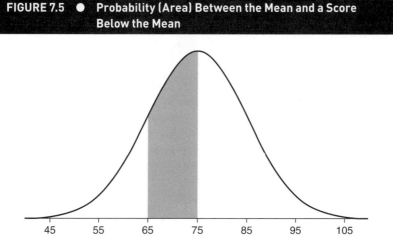

the curve, then since the normal distribution is symmetric, 34.13% of the area falls between one standard deviation and the mean on the right side. So, we know that in normal distributions, 68.26% of a distribution will fall within one standard deviation of the mean.

What if that score is higher than the mean? So, let's find the proportion of students whose scores are between 75 and 80 (see Figure 7.6).

c.   Convert 80 to a z score: $(80 - 75)/10 = .5$

d.   Look for .5 in the table (result in column B): .1915. This reveals that 19.15% of the area under the curve (and proportion of scores) lies between 75 and 80.

2.   What is the probability of falling into the interval between two scores (neither of which is the mean)?

What if the scores are on the same side of the mean (either both greater than or both less than the mean)? So, what proportion of the distribution lies between 80 and 85?

a.   Convert 80 and 85 to z scores: .5 and 1.

b.   Find the areas in column B of the standard normal table, then subtract the smaller from the larger, giving you .1499. As such, represented in Figure 7.7, 14.99% of the distribution falls between 80 and 85.

What if the scores are on opposite sides of the mean (one score is higher than the mean and one score is lower than the mean)? Let's calculate the proportion of the distribution between 70 and 85.

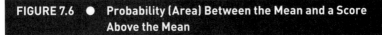

FIGURE 7.6 ● **Probability (Area) Between the Mean and a Score Above the Mean**

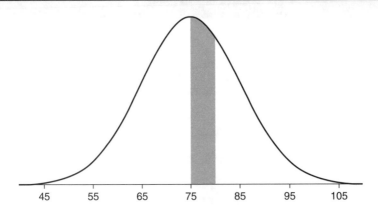

45   55   65   75   85   95   105

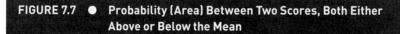

FIGURE 7.7 ● Probability (Area) Between Two Scores, Both Either Above or Below the Mean

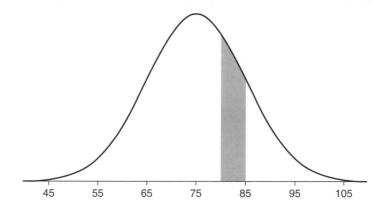

FIGURE 7.8 ● Probability (Area) Between Two Scores, One Above and One Below the Mean

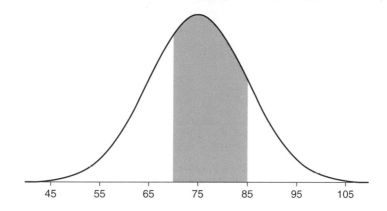

   c. Convert 70 and 85 to z scores: −.5 and 1.

   d. Find the areas in column B for each of these z scores, then add them together, giving you .5328, as seen in Figure 7.8.

3. What is the probability of falling into the interval above a particular score? What proportion of students had scores 90 and above?

   Convert 90 to a z score (1.5), then look up the value in column C: .0668, so 6.68% of students scored 90 or above (see Figure 7.9).

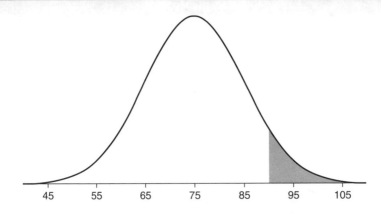

FIGURE 7.9 ● Probability (Area) Beyond a Score: Above

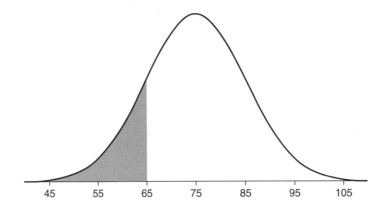

FIGURE 7.10 ● Probability (Area) Beyond a Score: Below

4. What is the probability of falling into the interval below a particular score? What proportion of students had scores below 65?

   Convert 65 to a z score (–1) and search for $z = 1$ in the standard normal table; the result will be in column C, .1587, as shown in Figure 7.10.

Working With the Standard Normal Distribution to Calculate z Scores, Raw Scores, and Percentiles

z Scores, Raw Scores

Suppose a graduate program to which you are applying requires you to be in the top 15% of your statistics class. With the knowledge of the distribution

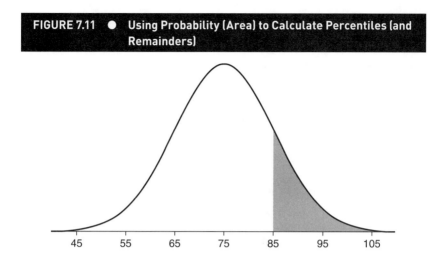

FIGURE 7.11 ● Using Probability (Area) to Calculate Percentiles (and Remainders)

(mean 75, standard deviation 10), you can estimate what score you need to earn in the class (and the associated z score).

Start by finding the area (.15) in column C of the table, then see what z score is associated with that area in column A: 1.04. Next, convert the z score to a raw score: 85.4, the score that bounds the upper 10% of the distribution (as shown in Figure 7.11).

Percentiles

A percentile represents the proportion of the distribution that falls below a particular score. So, if you need to find the percentile rank of a score, you are looking to find the area under the curve to the left of that raw score. For scores less than the mean, it's one step: look up the z score and see the area in column C. For scores greater than the mean use the result in column B and add that to .5 (to account for the left half of the area under the curve to the left of the mean).

Confidence Intervals

A **confidence interval** is the interval within which the researcher believes the population parameter will fall. The likelihood, expressed as a percentage or a probability, that a specified interval will contain a population parameter is known as the confidence level.

95% confidence level—there is a .95 probability that a specified interval *does* contain the population mean. In other words, there are 5 chances out of 100 (or 1 chance out of 20) that the interval *does not* contain the population mean.

99% confidence level—there is 1 chance out of 100 that the interval *does not* contain the population mean.

Constructing a Confidence Interval

The sample mean is the point estimate of the population mean. This point estimate establishes the middle point of the confidence interval; this is always the case, regardless of the confidence level.

The sample standard deviation is the point estimate of the population standard deviation. Knowing the standard error of the mean makes it possible to calculate the probability that an interval created around the point estimate contains the actual population parameter. This is usually done for the mean, but this can be done for other population parameters as well.

The goal is to construct an interval around the sample statistic (mean) within which you believe the population parameter (mean) will fall. The confidence level represents how sure, or confident, you are that the population mean is, in fact, contained within that interval. See Figure 7.12, where the sample mean serves as the point estimate for the population mean.

Larger intervals will result in greater confidence that a point is contained within that interval since the interval is larger and less precise than one that is smaller. So, if you cast a larger net, you are more likely to catch the fish, but you will need that bigger net. In the case of confidence intervals, the larger net means you will need a larger interval. Something to consider is that at what point will the interval become too large to be useful?

Shorter confidence intervals will result in lower levels of confidence because the interval is shorter and therefore more precise. The smaller interval is useful in that it makes a more narrow prediction, but if the level of confidence is too low, at what point is this little more than a guess?

FIGURE 7.12 ● Estimating the Population Mean From the Sample Mean

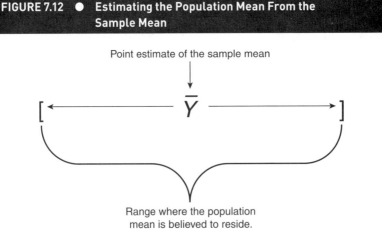

Point estimate of the sample mean

$\overline{Y}$

Range where the population mean is believed to reside.

There is definitely a philosophical balance to be considered between the size of the interval and the degree of confidence. Holding all other things constant, ceteris paribus, each of these is related to each other. Often, the discipline of study will dictate the confidence interval, and therefore, the size of the interval simply follows from that. Other times, there may be some flexibility. It is in that case that, as a researcher, you must consider the value of precision versus level of certainty.

Standard Error

In order to calculate a confidence interval, we need to incorporate some information about the distribution; this is done by utilizing the **standard error**, which is the standard deviation of a sampling distribution of sample means. The formula for the standard error is as follows:

$$\bar{y} = \frac{y}{\sqrt{N}}$$

This formula is rarely used in practice. Since the standard deviation of the population is typically not known, we are not able to calculate the standard error. If the standard deviation of the population were known, then it seems reasonable to assert that we would also already know the mean of the population.

Instead, we can use the standard deviation of the sample. When using the sample standard deviation, we no longer have calculated the standard error itself, but now we have calculated the **estimated standard error**, as seen in the following equation:

$$\bar{y} = \frac{y}{\sqrt{N}} \rightarrow = s_{\bar{y}}\left(\frac{s_Y}{\sqrt{N}}\right)$$

Calculating a Confidence Interval

In order to calculate a confidence interval, use the equation presented below. (Note that it makes use of the estimated standard error from the previous section.)

$$CI = \bar{Y} \pm z\left(s_{\bar{y}}\right)$$

where

$\bar{Y}$ = sample mean (estimate of m)

z = z score for one-half the acceptable error

$s_{\bar{y}}$ = estimated standard error

The value included in the equation for z represents one-half of the acceptable error, since the population parameter could be either larger than or smaller

TABLE 7.2 ● Confidence Levels Table	
90%	1.65
95%	1.96
99%	2.58

than the sample statistic. So half of the error will be calculated above the sample statistic, and half will be calculated below.

Expanding the estimated error to its components (the sample standard deviation divided by the square root of the sample size), we have the following equation:

$$\bar{Y} \pm z\left(\frac{s_Y}{\sqrt{N}}\right)$$

Confidence level: Increasing our confidence level from 95% to 99% means we are *less* willing to draw the wrong conclusion; we take a 1% risk (rather than 5%) that the specified interval does not contain the true population mean.

If we reduce our risk of being wrong, then we need a wider range of values, so the interval becomes *less* precise.

Confidence Interval Width

$$\bar{Y} \pm z\left(\frac{s_Y}{\sqrt{N}}\right)$$

Sample size: Larger samples result in smaller standard errors, and therefore sampling distributions that are more clustered around the population mean. A more closely clustered sampling distribution indicates that our confidence intervals will be narrower and more precise. Sample size is something that the researcher does have control over, though this is often tied to budget, time, and other resources.

$$\bar{Y} \pm z\left(\frac{s_Y}{\sqrt{N}}\right)$$

Standard deviation: Smaller sample standard deviations result in smaller, more precise confidence intervals. Unlike sample size and confidence level, the researcher plays absolutely no role in determining the standard deviation of a sample.

Confidence Intervals for Proportions

Using the central limit theorem (see Chapter 4), we can estimate the standard error of a proportion. A sampling distribution of proportions is approximately normal, with a mean, μ_p, equal to the population proportion, π, and with a standard error of proportions that is equal to

$$\mu_p = \sqrt{\frac{(\pi)(1-\pi)}{N}}$$

Be careful with this formula. In this case, π does not refer to the constant (3.14 . . .), but rather is a variable representing the proportion as a parameter in the population.

Again, we typically will not know the proportion and therefore the standard error of proportions, so we use the estimated standard error of proportions, as shown:

$$s_p = \sqrt{\frac{(p)(1-p)}{N}}$$

Above, p represents the proportion statistic computed for the sample. N, of course, represents the sample size.

The proportion sample statistic is a point estimate and serves as the middle point of the confidence interval. The confidence interval around the proportion can then be computed as follows:

$$p \pm z(s_p)$$

where

p = observed sample proportion (estimate of π)

z = z score for one-half the acceptable error

s_p = estimated standard error of the proportion

Answer to Quick Learning Check

Answer to quick learning check from earlier in the chapter: Since the standard deviation is equal to the square root of the variance, and in this case the standard deviation is equal to 10, then the variance must be equal to 100. The square root of the variance (100) = 10.

Terms

confidence interval 107	standard error 109
estimated standard error 109	z score (standard score) 97

Hypothesis Testing and Statistical Significance

Chapter 1 introduced the topic of inductive research—the process of testing a hypothesis to make general claims about the social world. As earlier chapters demonstrated, a hypothesis is a testable statement about the relationship between variables. Based on theory and logic, researchers set up expectations about the social world. Data are then collected from a sample, and statistical procedures are used to test those expectations and make inferences about larger populations. This chapter focuses on the logic of hypothesis testing and several tests of statistical significance. However, one must first understand the terms and conventions used by social science researchers when testing hypotheses.

Null and Alternative Hypotheses

As mentioned, explanatory and inductive research designs involve testing hypotheses. When the results of a research project are produced, researchers interpret their findings and then make a statement about the null hypothesis. The **null hypothesis (H_0)** suggests that a relationship, change, or effect *does not appear to exist* between the study's variables.[1] In other words, the independent variable does not exert a substantial influence on the dependent variable. By making a statement about the null hypothesis, researchers are providing

---

[1] The null hypothesis is sometimes referred to as the "no change hypothesis" or the "no effect hypothesis." The alternative hypothesis is sometimes referred to as the research hypothesis, represented as H_r or H_1.

support for their alternative hypothesis. The **alternative hypothesis (H_a)** is the opposite of the null hypothesis; this is a statement that there *is* a relationship between the independent variable(s) and the dependent variable. The following statements are examples of a null and alternative hypothesis.

Null Hypothesis (H_0): There is *no* difference in number of friends between men and women.

This null hypothesis is essentially proposing that the difference in number of friends between men and women is zero—this is the same as saying that gender and number of friends are not related. The population mean, which is estimated based on the sample mean, for number of women's friends (μ_1) is *the same* as the population mean for the number of men's friends (μ_2). The null hypothesis can also be stated in the following format: $\mu_1 = \mu_2$.

Nondirectional Alternative Hypothesis (H_a): There is a difference in number of friends between men and women.

This alternative hypothesis proposes that the difference in number of friends between men and women is *not* zero, which can also be presented as $\mu_1 \neq \mu_2$. In other words, some relationship *does* exist between the two variables: gender—the independent variable—has some effect on one's number of friends—the dependent variable. This framing is an example of a **nondirectional alternative hypothesis**, which is usually proposed when a researcher does not have a theoretical basis to present a more specific directional hypothesis.

If you have reason to believe that women, on average, have more friends than men, then you would propose this expected difference in the following **directional alternative hypothesis**, which reflects that difference:

Directional Alternative Hypothesis (H_a): Women have more friends than do men ($\mu_1 > \mu_2$).

The actual procedures used to test such a hypothesis and the notation used to describe them are covered later in this chapter. For now, it is important to focus on the language used in the hypothesis testing process.

Determination About the Null Hypothesis

When interpreting the results of a statistical analysis, researchers *make a determination about the null hypothesis* based on their results. This is the conventional way of making a statement supporting or contradicting the alternative hypothesis. If the results show support for the alternative hypothesis, the conventional language researchers use is that they "**reject the null hypothesis.**" Since the null hypothesis suggests that no effect exists between two variables, this notion is rejected when a relationship is present. On the other hand, if the results provide too little or no support for the alternative hypothesis, then researchers would "**fail to reject the null hypothesis.**" This is tricky language—the expression basically states that the researcher is unable to reject the notion that no relationship exists.

Researchers are often interested in rejecting the null hypothesis, which means that a relationship *does* exist between two variables (i.e., they reject the hypothesis that no relationship exists). Using the hypothesis examples above, imagine a researcher collects and analyzes data and concludes that she "rejects the null hypothesis." This means that she found that a relationship exists between gender and number of friends (i.e., one gender has more friends than the other). On the other hand, if she found that no difference exists, then she would "fail to reject the null hypothesis."

It is important to remember that *there are never absolutes in scientific research*. When interpreting the results of a statistical analysis, it is crucial to avoid definitive conclusions. One common remark in student papers is "Therefore, I have *proved* my hypothesis." Instead of making such absolute determinations, researchers use hedge language to highlight how *confident* they are about their research findings. The criteria for confidently supporting an alternative hypothesis are discussed in the next section.

Statistical Significance

Type I and Type II Errors

Since there is no way to ever be completely confident in the results of a study, researchers accept—but try to reduce—the probability of error in their conclusions. One type of error is made when a researcher rejects the null hypothesis (states there is a relationship) but the null hypothesis is true (there is no relationship in real life)—this type of error is known as a **Type I error**. A Type I error is also referred to as a "false positive" since the data do show a relationship (positive), but this conclusion is false. Another way researchers might draw an erroneous conclusion would be failing to reject the null hypothesis when the null hypothesis is false, which is known as a **Type II error**. Type II errors are also known as "false negative" errors since the researcher *does not* find a relationship (negative), but that conclusion is false.

These errors do not occur because of some statistical oversight or mistake made by the researcher; rather, they are errors about the applicability of the findings in real life. Therefore, it could never be definitively established whether a null or alternative hypothesis is "true" in real life. The types of error exist so that researchers can present how confident they are in their results despite the probability of error.

As shown in Table 8.1, the two types of error cannot be present at the same time. This table presents the four possible outcomes of a hypothesis test based on the decision that is made about the null hypothesis. In cells (b) and (c), there are no errors made. The researcher is correct in either rejecting the null hypothesis (b) or failing to reject the null hypothesis (c). On the other hand,

TABLE 8.1 ● The Four Possible Outcomes of a Research Design		
	Research Conclusion	
Reality	**Reject H_0**	**Fail to reject H_0**
H_0 is true	(a) Type I error	(b) No error
H_0 is false	(c) No error	(d) Type II error

cells (a) and (d) represent the errors that might be made. Type I error (a) is erroneously rejecting a null hypothesis that is true—a false positive. Type II error is reflected in cell (d), which is failing to reject a null hypothesis when the null hypothesis is false—a false negative.

In order to assess the probability of making a Type I error, researchers use tests of statistical significance, this topic is covered throughout the remainder of this chapter. Issues surrounding Type II errors are addressed in Chapter 10, which covers power analysis and effect size. For the following sections, it is important to recognize that (a) Type I errors occur when researchers reject the null hypothesis but the null hypothesis is true, and (b) Type II errors occur when researchers fail to reject the null hypothesis but the null hypothesis is false. The following sections explore the criteria researchers use to make determinations about Type I errors and draw conclusions about the null hypothesis.

Alpha

To address the possibility of a Type I error, researchers decide on the amount of probable error they are willing to handle if they reject the null hypothesis and the null hypothesis is true. This criterion is represented by the term *alpha* (α). **Alpha** is the cutoff probability a researcher allows for erroneously rejecting the null hypothesis when the null hypothesis is true. The standard levels of alpha conventionally used in social science research are .05, .01, and .001. These probabilities respectively correspond to allowing for a 5%, 1%, or .1% chance of erroneously rejecting the null hypothesis (i.e., making a Type I error).

In any given test of statistical significance, the estimated probability of making a Type I error is known as the ***p* value**. If the *p* value is lower than the alpha cutoff, a researcher can be confident that the results are **statistically significant** at that level.[2] However, if the *p* value is higher than the alpha, then the researcher has a higher chance than anticipated of being wrong if he or she

---

[2] Rather than present the individual *p* value for all statistical analyses, social science researchers use the following conventions to indicate the level of statistical significance when presenting their results. A single asterisk (*) is used next to a statistic to denote that the result is significant at the .05 level of alpha. Two asterisks (**) are used to indicate that a relationship is significant at the .01 level of alpha. Three asterisks (***) are used to indicate that the result is significant at the .001 level of alpha. Additional symbols can also denote when a result is significant at higher levels of alpha (e.g., † is sometimes used to represent a relationship that is significant at the .10 level). However, this is allowing for a 10% chance of making a Type I error, which is often considered too large.

rejects the null hypothesis. Therefore, researchers reject the null hypothesis if the probability of making a Type I error (p value) is lower than the cutoff established (alpha). In this case, the researcher can conclude that the hypothesized relationship is statistically significant at that level of alpha.

For example, the researcher testing the null hypothesis that there is *no* gender difference in number of friends sets an alpha of .05. This means he is willing to reject the null hypothesis only when there is *at most* a 5% chance of making a Type I error. If the results of his statistical analysis yield a p value of .04, then he can confidently reject the null hypothesis because *the probability of making a Type I error is less than the alpha of .05*. He can therefore conclude that there is a statistically significant relationship between gender and number of friends at the .05 level of alpha. However, since the p value is .04, this means there is still a 4% chance of making a Type I error. The common notation for this finding is $p < .05$, where p stands for "probability of making a Type I error." In other words, the *probability of making a Type I error is less than the predetermined alpha level of .05*. However, in order to provide more insight into their results, some choose to sidestep this convention and present the actual p value for all findings (rather than using .05, .01, and .001 cutoffs).

It is important to note that just because a result is statistically significant, it does not always have practical importance. Providing support that a relationship exists between variables should never imply that the relationship is substantively meaningful. Taking the previous example, finding a statistically significant relationship between gender and number of friends simply means that the difference between men and women *is not zero*. Whether this effect has practical or theoretical value is a separate issue, explored in Chapter 10. The next section explores the **test statistic**—the statistical value used to make a determination about the null hypothesis.

Test Statistic Distributions

In order to interpret the results of a hypothesis test, researchers draw on test statistics, which are numerical values that represent the relationship between variables. Depending on the statistical test, test statistics all have a different distribution. Researchers are most interested in finding out where a given statistic falls within a distribution of values. Each distribution is separated into two parts, the region of rejection and the nonrejection region.

If a test statistic falls within the **nonrejection region**, then a researcher fails to reject the null hypothesis. If, however, the test statistic falls outside of the nonrejection region—in the **region of rejection**—then a researcher rejects the null hypothesis.[3] The point where one region ends and the other begins depends on the alpha. The first panel of Figure 8.1 presents an example of these regions for a normal (z) distribution with an alpha level of .05. The regions of rejection are located in either extreme of the distribution (i.e., the upper and lower tails). If you were to use a larger alpha (e.g., .10), that

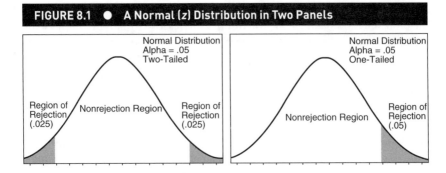

FIGURE 8.1 ● A Normal (z) Distribution in Two Panels

Note: The α is .05 for both distributions. The left panel illustrates the nonrejection region and regions of rejection for a *two-tailed* (directional) hypothesis. The right panel illustrates a single region of rejection for the same distribution. This is an example of the critical region for a one-tailed (nondirectional) hypothesis.

would lead to a higher probability of rejecting the null hypothesis and, in turn, a larger region of rejection.

In Figure 8.1, the alpha level was set at .05, which means the regions of rejection are located in the uppermost 2.5% and the lowermost 2.5%, totaling .05 or 5%. This is an example of a **two-tailed test**, where a researcher is comparing the test statistic against rejection regions on both sides of the distribution. A two-tailed distribution is used to test a nondirectional hypothesis (e.g., if the researcher has no reason to expect the test statistic to fall in one tail of the distribution or the other). However, not all hypothesis tests compare a test statistic against rejection regions in both tails.

When a researcher proposes a directional hypothesis, which can happen with a *t* test (discussed later), the region of rejection will be reflected on only one side of the distribution—this is known as a **one-tailed test**. The tail where the region of rejection exists depends on the hypothesis. The second panel of Figure 8.1 presents an example of the region of rejection for a one-tailed test of a directional hypothesis. In this distribution, the region of rejection is located only in the right tail. Note that in this panel, which still uses a .05 alpha level, all 5% of the region of rejection is located in the uppermost tail of the distribution. In the first panel with a two-tailed test, the alpha level was distributed evenly to both sides.

Choosing a Test of Statistical Significance

Since, up to this point, the chapter has focused on introducing the major concepts and conventions for interpreting statistical results, some of the terms

---

[3] The region of rejection is also sometimes referred to as the critical region.

might have seemed vague. However, once hypotheses and alpha levels have been established, the next step is to identify an appropriate statistical test for a hypothesis. This will ultimately lead to obtaining a test statistic, which can be compared to the test's distribution.

When choosing a test of statistical significance, the most appropriate test will depend upon a number of factors, including the levels of measurement for the independent and dependent variables. Statistical procedures also rest on assumptions about the data that must be met in order to accurately interpret the results of the test. For example, if you were to interpret the mean score for gender in your study, this would be an erroneous interpretation of central tendency because it violates the assumption that a variable must be interval/ratio in order to have a meaningful mean. Doing so for a nominal variable produces an arbitrary number.

There are two different types of statistical tests, parametric and nonparametric. The distinction between them is rooted in their assumptions about the data. **Parametric tests** are procedures where information about a sample is used to estimate the population characteristics. Accordingly, there are strict assumptions about the distribution of the data. These tests are usually most appropriate when the data are interval/ratio level and normally distributed. On the other hand, **nonparametric tests**—also known as distribution-free statistics—do not use sample data to approximate a larger sample. As such, these procedures have fewer assumptions about the distribution. Therefore, if you have categorical (nominal, ordinal, or dichotomous) or non-normally distributed interval/ratio data, then nonparametric statistics are usually an appropriate approach.

When planning to test a hypothesis, make sure to take into account some of the issues discussed in earlier chapters. First, in order to get a sense of how the data are distributed, check descriptive statistics and examine data visualizations. Check frequencies to get a sense of the amount of missing data—if certain variables are missing a great deal of data, that could influence the interpretation. Each of the next several sections details commonly employed tests of statistical significance. The first procedure, chi-square, is a nonparametric test. The second and third tests, t test and analysis of variance, are parametric tests.

The Chi-Square Test of Independence (χ^2)

The **chi-square test of independence**, which is represented by the notation χ^2, is a nonparametric test to explore the relationship between two categorical variables.[4] The test examines whether two nominal variables are related. The tests can also be used for ordinal-level or even grouped interval/ratio-level data;

---

[4] The "chi" part of chi-square is pronounced "khy" and rhymes with "eye." It is based on the Greek letter *chi* (χ).

however, the ordered nature of the data is not taken into account (i.e., the variables are "treated" like a nominal variable).[5]

In the test of independence, the null hypothesis states that two variables are **independent**; in other words, they are unrelated and operate independently of each other. Conversely, the alternative hypothesis proposes that two variables are related in some way. Because the data are treated as nominal, there is no directional hypothesis. There is also no distinction between the independent variable and dependent variable.

The hypotheses for the chi-square test of independence simply state whether or not the two variables are related. For example, a researcher is interested in examining whether there is a relationship between gender and whether an individual considers his or her family an important source of stress (famstress). The null hypothesis is that no relationship exists between gender and famstress. The alternative hypothesis is that gender and famstress are somehow related.

Observed and Expected Frequencies

To test a hypothesis using the chi-square test of independence, a set of **observed frequencies**—the frequencies you observe in your data—is compared to a set of **expected frequencies**—the frequencies you would expect if the variables were independent. Both sets of frequencies are presented in contingency tables, which were discussed in Chapter 4. Observed frequencies are contingency tables that are based on the *actual* (observed) data. They present the frequency of one variable across different categories of another. Table 8.2 presents observed frequencies for family stress presented separately for men and women. For assistance interpreting the information presented in the contingency table, refer to Chapter 4.

The expected frequencies are calculated for each cell based on the row and column totals in the observed data. The formula to calculate these frequencies is shown in Formula 8.1. The resulting "expected model" is a hypothetical distribution that would exist *if the two variables are independent*. The frequencies and percentages in Table 8.3 are what the data would look like if equal percentages of men and women reported that their family is an important source of stress. Decimal places are common for expected frequencies because this is only a hypothetical distribution. These equal percentages would mean that gender and famstress were completely independent.

Formula 8.1 Expected Cell Frequency

$$f_e = \frac{(row\ total) \bullet (column\ total)}{N}$$

---

[5] There is a second—less common—type of χ^2 test known as the chi-square goodness-of-fit test. The goodness-of-fit test, also known as a univariate chi-square test, compares the frequency distribution for a single nominal variable to a hypothetical distribution.

TABLE 8.2 ● A Contingency Table with *Observed* Frequencies for sex and famstress

famstress * sex Contingency Table (Observed Values)

		Sex		
		Male	Female	Total
Relationships with family members bring a lot of stress	No	434	394	828
	Yes	89	83	172
Total		523	477	1,000

TABLE 8.3 ● A Contingency Table with *Expected* Frequencies for sex and famstress

famstress * sex Contingency Table (Expected Values)

		Sex		
		Male	Female	Total
Relationships with family members bring a lot of stress	No	433.0	395.0	828.0
	Yes	90.0	82.0	172.0
Total		523.0	477.0	1,000.0

Chi-Square Test Statistic

The primary objective of this test of statistical significance is to assess how closely the observed model (Table 8.2) resembles the expected model. If the observed frequencies are extremely similar to the expected model (Table 8.3), then the variables could be independent. On the other hand, if the two sets of frequencies are extremely different, the test of independence assesses (a) how different and (b) if the differences could be based on chance. In other words, the test examines whether the difference between the observed and expected frequencies is large enough to reject the null hypothesis. The formula to determine the chi-square test statistic is shown in Formula 8.2.

Formula 8.2 Chi-Square Test Statistic (χ^2)

$$\chi^2 = \sum \frac{(f_o - f_e)^2}{f_e}$$

The resulting statistic is known as the **obtained value** of chi-square. Think of this numerical value as a representation of how different the observed table is from the expected table. If the chi-square test statistic value is 0.00, then the observed model is basically the same as—or at least *very close to*—the expected model. Since the expected model reflects complete independence, an obtained value of 0.00 would indicate that the observed model (based on the data) is also independent. Accordingly, greater differences between the observed and expected models mean a larger obtained value.

Chi-Square Distribution and Degrees of Freedom

In order to determine whether the test statistic is larger than one might expect based on chance alone, the test statistic must be compared to a known distribution of chi-square values based on chance. The test statistic is compared to such a distribution, the **chi-square distribution**. Since the value of chi-square is never less than zero, the distribution is asymmetrical (positively skewed). For this reason, researchers almost always focus on the one-tailed test of independence.

The shape of the chi-square distribution is determined largely by the number of degrees of freedom in the analysis. **Degrees of freedom** are the number of cells that can vary based on the row and column totals. There is a different chi-square distribution for every degree of freedom. The calculation of the number of degrees of freedom for chi-square is based on the formula shown in Formula 8.3. In order to make a determination about the test statistic and the distribution, a chi-square table is used (along with the degrees of freedom and alpha) to retrieve a critical value of chi-square.

Formula 8.3 Chi-Square Degrees of Freedom (df)

$$df = (\# \text{ Rows} - 1) \times (\# \text{ Columns} - 1)$$

Chi-Square Table

The chi-square table provides a **critical value**, which is where the nonrejection region ends and the region of rejection begins for different degrees of freedom (distributions) and levels of alpha. In order to make a determination about the null hypothesis, you need to compare the test statistic (obtained value) to the critical value found in this table (see Appendix C). For example, with one degree of freedom, the critical value of chi-square at the .05 level of alpha is 3.84 (see Table 8.4). If the obtained value (i.e., chi-square test statistic)

TABLE 8.4 ● A Small Section of the χ^2 Table

Degrees of Freedom	Percentage Points of the Chi-Square Distribution								
	Probability of a larger value of χ^2								
	0.99	0.95	0.90	0.75	0.50	0.25	0.10	0.05	0.01
1	0.000	0.004	0.016	0.102	0.455	1.32	2.71	3.84	6.63
2	0.020	0.103	0.211	0.575	1.386	2.77	4.61	5.99	9.21
3	0.115	0.352	0.584	1.212	2.366	4.11	6.25	7.81	11.34
4	0.297	0.711	1.064	1.923	3.357	5.39	7.78	9.49	13.28
5	0.554	1.145	1.610	2.675	4.351	6.63	9.24	11.07	15.09

is higher than the critical value, you reject the null hypothesis. The conclusion in this case would be that there is a statistically significant relationship between the two variables.

If the obtained value is smaller than the critical value, you fail to reject the null hypothesis. If you fail to reject the null hypothesis, you can check the table to see if you could reject the null hypothesis at a higher alpha level. Doing so leads to a lower critical value (e.g., with an alpha of .10, the critical value is 2.7); however, rejecting the null hypothesis at the .10 level of alpha also means a higher probability of making a Type I error. Since most statistical analysis software produces this information without the need for the table, the next section ties everything together with the values provided in common social science statistical applications.

Chi-Square Output and Interpretation

When interpreting the results of chi-square analyses, it is important to remember that the relationship tested in a chi-square is only *correlational*—no statements can be made about a causal relationship. Recall from Chapter 2 that a correlation is only one of three criteria establishing a causal relationship. Therefore, chi-square results must *always* be framed as correlational. Additionally, when writing up results of any statistical analysis, it is important to *at least* include information about the hypothesis, test statistic, degrees of freedom, and *p* value. The format for presenting test results varies based on professional standards; be sure to check the style guide conventionally used in your discipline (e.g., ASA, APA, Chicago, MLA) before writing up results. The following three examples are based on the analysis of a nonrandom sample of 1,000 U.S. adult men and women.

Example 1: Gender and Family Stress

Table 8.5 contains values that are commonly provided in output produced by statistical analysis applications. This example examines the relationship between gender and reporting that family is an important source of stress (famstress). Therefore, the null hypothesis states that gender and family stress are unrelated. The alternative hypothesis is that gender and family stress are related in some way. The table shows the full *N* of the study along with details about the missing data. The lower part of the table shows the chi-square value of .026 (a) with 1 degree of freedom (b). As Figure 8.2 illustrates, this value would be in the *nonrejection region*. In support of this, the *p* value reflected in the output is .873 (c), which means if we were to reject the null hypothesis based on the results of this analysis, there would be an 87% chance we would be making a Type I error. Therefore, based on the information in the table, we fail to reject the null hypothesis.

An example of how to write up these results would be to state, "A chi-square test of independence examined the relationship between gender and whether

TABLE 8.5 ● Output From a Chi-Square Test of Independence Between the Variables sex and famstress					
Chi-Square Tests					
	Value	df	Asymp. Sig. (2-sided)	Exact Sig. (2-sided)	Exact Sig. (1-sided)
Pearson chi-square	.026[a]	1	.873		
Continuity correction[b]	.006	1	.939		
Likelihood ratio	.026	1	.873		
Fisher's exact test				.933	.469
Linear-by-linear association	.026	1	.873		
N of valid cases	1,000				

[a] Zero cells (0.0%) have expected count less than 5. The minimum expected count is 82.04.
[b] Computed only for a 2 × 2 table.

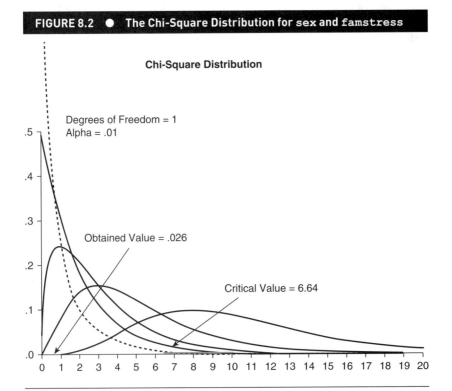

FIGURE 8.2 ● The Chi-Square Distribution for sex and famstress

Chi-Square Distribution

Degrees of Freedom = 1
Alpha = .01

Obtained Value = .026

Critical Value = 6.64

Note: The distribution has one degree of freedom because it is a 2 × 2 contingency table. The other distribution markers are the distributions for tests with more degrees of freedom. With an α of .01, the critical region (region of rejection) begins on the x-axis at 6.64. Since the test statistic had a value of .026, χ^2 does not fall within the rejection region.

or not an individual reported that his or her family is an important source of stress (famstress). The null hypothesis states that gender and family stress are not related. Based on the analysis, we fail to reject the null hypothesis. The results suggest that there is no significant relationship between gender and family stress ($\chi^2 = .025$, $df = 1$, $p = .87$)."

Example 2: Gender and Chore Stress

The following analysis is based on a chi-square test of independence using the same sample as above. The analysis explores whether or not gender is related to feeling that chores are an important source of stress (chorestress). The null hypothesis is that gender and chorestress are independent (i.e., not associated). The alternative hypothesis is that the two variables are associated (i.e., not independent). Table 8.6 presents information from the statistical analysis. The chi-square test statistic is 28.3 with 1 degree of freedom. The *p* value listed is .000, which indicates that rejecting the null hypothesis would lead to less than a 0.1% chance of making a Type I error. Based on this information, a researcher would reject the null hypothesis. The results suggest that there is a statistically significant relationship between gender and reporting that chores are an important source of stress ($\chi^2 = 28.3$, $df = 1$, $p < .001$).

Example 3: Gender and Chore Stress by Age Group

When the sample size is large enough to accommodate large tables, chi-square analyses can also be performed to test the relationship between two variables across multiple groups. For example, Table 8.7 presents the results of three chi-square tests of independence between gender and chore stress (chorestress). The results are presented for different age groups—early adulthood, midlife, and older adulthood. In a contingency table, observed and expected frequencies would be presented in a $2 \times 2 \times 3$ table; however, the chi-square

TABLE 8.6 ● Information Regarding the Relationship Between sex and chorestress

chorestress * sex Contingency Table			Sex		
			Male	Female	Total
Household chores bring a lot of stress	No	Count	439	333	772
		Expected count	403.8	368.2	772.0
	Yes	Count	84	144	228
		Expected count	119.2	108.8	228.0
Total		Count	523	477	1,000
		Expected count	523.0	477.0	1,000.0

(Continued)

TABLE 8.6 ● (Continued)

Chi-Square Tests					
	Value	df	Asymp. Sig. (2-sided)	Exact Sig. (2-sided)	Exact Sig. (1-sided)
Pearson chi-square	28.288[a]	1	.000		
Continuity correction[b]	27.491	1	.000		
Likelihood ratio	28.461	1	.000		
Fisher's exact test				.000	.000
Linear-by-linear association	28.259	1	.000		
N of valid cases	1,000				

Note: The top panel provides the observed and expected frequencies in a single contingency table. The bottom panel provides the results of a chi-square test of independence.

[a] Zero cells (0.0%) have expected count less than 5. The minimum expected count is 108.76.

[b] Computed only for a 2×2 table.

TABLE 8.7 ● Output for a Chi-Square Test of Independence Between gender and chorestress Across Three Different Age Groups (agegroup)

Ages Grouped		Value	df	Asymp. Sig. (2-sided)
Early adulthood (18–34)	Pearson chi-square	7.862	1	.005
	N of valid cases	313		
Adulthood (35–64)	Pearson chi-square	11.328	1	.001
	N of valid cases	635		
Older adulthood (65+)	Pearson chi-square	2.641	1	.104
	N of valid cases	52		
Total	Pearson chi-square	28.288	1	.000
	N of valid cases	1,000		

statistic is calculated separately for each of the three groups. As such, the expected and observed frequencies are compared separately for young adults, midlife adults, and older adults.

The results of this analysis indicate that there is a significant relationship between gender and chore stress among young adults ($\chi^2 = 7.9$, $df = 1$, $p < .01$) and midlife adults ($\chi^2 = 11.3$, $df = 1$, $p < .001$). However, there is not a statistically significant relationship among older adults ($\chi^2 = 2.6$, $df = 1$, $p = 0.10$).

Chi-Square Overview

The chi-square test of independence is used to test the relationship between two nominal variables and make inferences about a larger population. The procedure can also be used for ordinal variables and interval/ratio variables collapsed into small groups, but the test of independence treats the categories as nominal. The test statistic (obtained value of chi-square) is a numerical representation of how the observed frequencies in the contingency table differ from a set of expected frequencies that would occur if the two variables were completely independent. The chi-square distribution is defined by the degrees of freedom, and the region of rejection is based on the critical value of chi-square, which is informed by the level of alpha. The obtained and critical values of chi-square are compared in order to make a determination about the null hypothesis.

Although chi-square is a nonparametric test, there are several assumptions about the data that can lead to erroneous results when violated. First, the *expected* frequency model should not contain cells with a frequency lower than 5. This is a common problem with very small samples or with nominal variables that have many categories, leading to large contingency tables.[6] In some cases, smaller groups can be collapsed into larger ones. At other times, statistical procedures (e.g., Fisher's exact test) might be employed to account for small sample sizes. Second, an individual must not be in more than one cell or group. This might be the case in an experimental design if you are interested in whether or not completing chores influences stress. This could occur if you (a) asked individuals whether or not chores cause them stress (chorestress1), then (b) observed individuals completing several hours of tedious chores, and then (c) asked the same individuals to report whether or not chores cause them stress (chorestress2). A chi-square test would be an inappropriate procedure to examine the relationship between chorestress1 and chorestress2 because the same individuals are in both groups. If, however, chorestress could be measured with an interval/ratio variable, a paired *t* test would be an appropriate design. This design is discussed briefly in the next section.

The Independent Samples *t* Test

The **independent samples *t* test** is a procedure used to assess whether or not a mean significantly differs between two independent groups.[7] In this

---

[6] While the test in these examples used 2 × 2 contingency tables (only two categories for each variable), the test of independence can also be conducted on nominal variables with many more categories (e.g., 2 × 3, 3 × 3, and so on). Having more rows and columns can lead to smaller expected frequencies, depending on the number of cells and the sample size. The number of rows and columns also influences the degrees of freedom and chi-square distribution.

[7] There are two other types of *t* tests, rooted in similar logic, that are not discussed in this section. First, a paired samples *t* test, or dependent samples *t* test, is a comparison of means for samples

context, the term *independent* means that the individuals in one group do not influence the selection of individuals into the other group.[8] To conduct a *t* test, the independent variable must be dichotomous (a variable with only two groups), and the dependent variable must be measured at the interval/ ratio level. This type of situation is common in social science research. For example, in survey-based research, the *t* test is often used to compare interval/ratio scores between two groups (e.g., men and women). In experimental research, the *t* test is useful when comparing the mean scores for experimental and control groups.

The *t* test is the first of two parametric tests discussed in this chapter. These tests have more assumptions regarding distribution and variance than the nonparametric chi-square test of independence. Three of the most important assumptions are that (a) the data are normally distributed for both populations; (b) there is **homogeneity of variance**, which means that the standard deviations are approximately equal for both populations; and (c) there are no extreme outliers in either group, which can be examined by looking at separate modified boxplots for men and women (see Chapter 5). While these assumptions are important, the *t* test will produce reasonably accurate results if violated—insofar as neither assumption is violated egregiously. However, if the data for either group are highly skewed and/or there are large differences in variance, then a different statistical test is more appropriate—perhaps a nonparametric test with fewer distribution assumptions.

Independent Samples *t*-Test Notation and Hypotheses

The hypotheses for an independent samples *t* test state whether there are expected differences between population means based on the sample means. While it is very likely that the two means will differ, the important part of the test is whether or not the difference *could be based on chance*. Since the *t* test is based on characteristics of two different populations and two different samples (and uses sample information to estimate population characteristics), there is a wider range of notation when calculating a *t* test (see Table 8.8).

The null hypothesis (H_0) states that there is *no* mean difference between Group 1 and Group 2—in other words, the difference between the two groups is zero. Because the μ (*mu*) symbol represents the population mean, the null

---

that are related in some way (e.g., a pretest and a posttest experimental design where Groups 1 and 2 are the same individuals). Second, the one-sample *t* test compares the mean of the sample to that of a larger population when the population mean is known.

[8] Independent samples *t* tests are also known by other names: *t* test for independent groups and two-sample *t* test.

TABLE 8.8 ●	Standard Statistical Notation Used in the Independent Samples *t* Test			
	Size	Mean	Standard Deviation	Variance
Population	N	μ	σ	σ^2
Group 1	n_1	$\bar{X}_1$	s_1	s_1^2
Group 2	n_2	$\bar{X}_2$	s_2	s_2^2

hypothesis can also be stated as $\mu_1 = \mu_2$. Saying much the same thing but framing it in terms of the *difference* between groups, we have the following: $\mu_1 - \mu_2 = 0$. A nondirectional (two-tailed) alternative hypothesis (H_a) is that the difference between the two groups is not zero, or $\mu_1 - \mu_2 \neq 0$.

However, the hypothesis can be directional—which also means that the *t* test can be one-tailed. Thus, a directional alternative hypothesis can be presented in different ways depending on which group is expected to be larger. For example, if you had reason to believe that the mean for Group 1 would be greater than that of Group 2, the hypothesis would be framed as follows:

H_a: The mean for Group 1 is greater than that of Group 2 ($\mu_1 > \mu_2$). In terms of difference between the groups, this is the same as saying that $\mu_1 - \mu_2 > 0$.

The directional hypothesis is always the opposite of the null hypothesis. Therefore, in the event that Group 2 is significantly larger than Group 1, you would still *fail to reject the null hypothesis* (conclude that there is *no difference*). This is because the region of rejection in a one-tailed test is present in the opposite tail. If the test statistic is located in the extreme of the *other* direction, it is still considered the nonrejection region, and you would fail to reject the null hypothesis. This might obscure otherwise significant and interesting differences between two groups, which is why some researchers have cautioned against using one-tailed *t* tests.

The Logic of the *t*-Test Statistic

The basic premise behind the *t*-test statistic is to compare distributions based on the difference between means. In the simplest terms, the logic is to calculate the **difference between means** by (a) randomly selecting a sample mean from Group 1, (b) randomly selecting a sample mean from Group 2, and (c) subtracting the sample mean from Group 2 from that of Group 1. Repeating this over and over again results in a distribution of the differences between means. Based on this process, the mathematical formula for finding the **obtained *t* statistic** (the test statistic) is shown in Formula 8.4.

Formula 8.4 t Statistic

$$t = \frac{\bar{X}_1 - \bar{X}_2}{se_{\bar{X}_1 - \bar{X}_2}}$$

The t statistic can be negative or positive. The t statistic can be thought of as a numerical representation of the difference between means. A test statistic of zero indicates that there is no difference in means between the two groups. The larger the absolute value of the t statistic (the farther it gets from zero on either side), the larger the difference between means and the smaller the probability of making a Type I error.

One-Tailed and Two-Tailed t Tests

Recall from earlier in the chapter that the region(s) of rejection in the t distribution depend upon whether the test is one-tailed or two-tailed. Two-tailed tests are associated with nondirectional alternative hypotheses, where the alternative hypothesis is that the group means are *different* ($\mu_1 \neq \mu_2$). Since you can reject the null hypothesis for a two-tailed test when the t statistic is positive *or* negative, the alpha and region of rejection are split evenly in the left and right tails. For example, with an alpha of .05, then .025 will be the cutoff for the region of rejection in the left tail and .025 will be the cutoff for the region of rejection in the right tail. If the absolute value of the t statistic falls within the rejection region in either the left tail or the right tail, we reject the null hypothesis and conclude that means for each group are significantly different. On the other hand, if the absolute value of the t statistic lies within the central nonrejection region of the distribution, we fail to reject the null hypothesis.

A one-tailed t test is based on a directional hypothesis, which means there is a proposed expectation about where (i.e., which tail) the region of rejection falls. Therefore, rather than splitting the alpha into two rejection regions, the region of rejection is in only one tail. A positive t statistic indicates that Group 1 is larger than Group 2 ($\mu_1 > \mu_2$), and a negative statistic indicates that Group 2 is larger than Group 1 ($\mu_2 > \mu_1$). Therefore, when conducting a one-tailed test, two pieces of information tell us whether or not we can reject the null hypothesis: the positive or negative sign of the t statistic, and whether or not it lies within the rejection region of the appropriate tail. However, if the t statistic is located in the extreme of the *opposite* direction than the one hypothesized, it would be considered the nonrejection region, and you would still fail to reject the null hypothesis. This is an important precaution against one-tailed hypotheses because it might lead a researcher to overlook otherwise significant differences between the groups.

The *t* Distribution and Degrees of Freedom

The distribution of the *t* test is known as the **t distribution**. Like the chi-square distribution, the number of degrees of freedom for the *t* statistic informs the shape of the distribution. The degrees of freedom for the *t* test are based on the number of scores that can vary if information on the mean is provided. In other words, if you have the mean, you can extrapolate from the data to determine a single missing score. Therefore, the total degrees of freedom for the *t* statistic is $N - 1$. The shape of the *t* distribution is more symmetrical than the chi distribution. However, it is more spread out and platykurtic when the sample is small. As the sample size increases, so do the degrees of freedom, and the *t* distribution tends toward a normal distribution—this is because there are more scores, which creates a more spread-out distribution.

The *t* Table

The *t* table (see Appendix B) presents the **t critical values**, which are based on characteristics of the study: the degrees of freedom, whether the test is one-tailed or two-tailed, and the alpha. The rows of the table provide different degrees of freedom—note that when the degrees of freedom become larger, the intervals between them increase. When selecting a number for degrees of freedom, if your exact number is not represented in the table, the conservative approach is to select the closest lower number (e.g., if you have 38 degrees of freedom and the table options list 30 or 40, you should select 30). Similar to other tests of statistical significance, once you have retrieved the critical value for your study, you compare it to the obtained *t* statistic (see Table 8.9). If the obtained value is higher than the critical value, you reject the null hypothesis. On the other hand, if the critical value is higher than the obtained value, you fail to reject the null hypothesis.

df/p	0.40	0.25	0.10	0.05	0.025	0.01
1	0.324920	1.000000	3.077684	6.313752	12.70620	31.82052
2	0.288675	0.816497	1.885618	2.919986	4.30265	6.96456
3	0.276671	0.764892	1.637744	2.353363	3.18245	4.54070
4	0.270722	0.740697	1.533206	2.131847	2.77645	3.74695
5	0.267181	0.726687	1.475884	2.015048	2.57058	3.36493
6	0.264835	0.717558	1.439756	1.943180	2.44691	3.14267

TABLE 8.9 ● A Small Section of the *t* Table

Independent Samples *t*-Test Output and Interpretation

When you interpret and write up the results of a *t* test, keep in mind that the results are correlational. As such, it is important to avoid making claims about causal relationships. Additionally, when discussing your results, be sure to include information about the hypothesis (and direction, if applicable), the test statistic, degrees of freedom, whether the test is one-tailed or two-tailed, and the *p* value. The next section applies actual data to the previous concepts to help you interpret the results of your own research. The following examples are based on the analysis of a nonrandom sample of 1,000 U.S. adult men and women.

Example 1: Gender and Number of Friends (Nondirectional)

The first example is based on gender—the dichotomous independent variable—and number of close friends (friendstotal)—the interval/ratio dependent variable. The null hypothesis states that there is no difference in mean number of close friends between men and women ($\mu_{men} = \mu_{women}$). There are a few reasons why men and women might have *different* numbers of close friends. However, it is less clear which group will have more close friends than the other. For this reason, the alternative hypothesis is non-directional. The alternative hypothesis states that there *is* a difference in the mean number of friends for men and women ($\mu_{men} \neq \mu_{women}$). Table 8.10 provides the information needed in order to make a decision about the null hypothesis.

In the table, there is information on the two groups in the independent variable—men are in Group 1 and women are in Group 2. This table allows for a quick assessment of subsample characteristics for each group: the size of each subsample ($n_1 = 523$, $n_2 = 477$); the means ($\bar{X}_1 = 8.2$, $\bar{X}_2 = 7.9$); and the standard deviations ($s_1 = 7.4$, $s_2 = 6.3$). Thus, you are able to quickly compare the size of each group and the groups' means, including which group's mean is larger.

The second part provides a section for Levene's Test. Recall from the beginning of this section that homogeneity of variance is an important assumption for the *t* test—Levene's Test checks whether this condition was met in the data. The result of the test determines which half of the output should be interpreted. Since the *p* value for Levene's Test is less than .05, the variance is *not the same* for both groups (i.e., the difference in variance for each group is not zero). Although this is a violation of the homogeneity of variances assumption, the results can instead be interpreted along the bottom row, which adjusts the results to correct for the violation.

In the next part of the table, the *t* statistic (a), 0.71, is very close to zero, suggesting that the mean difference between the two groups is not very large. The *p* value (c) indicates whether or not we reject the hypothesis. Since the *p* value (.48) is beyond the .05 threshold, we fail to reject the null hypothesis.

TABLE 8.10 ●	Results of an Independent Samples *t* Test for the Variables sex and friendstotal

Group Statistics

	Sex	N	Mean	Std. Deviation	Std. Error Mean
Total close friends	Male	523	8.17	7.433	.325
	Female	477	7.87	6.289	.288

Independent Samples Test

Dependent Variable: Total Close Friends	Levene's Test F	Sig.	*t*	*df*	Sig. (2-tailed)	Mean Difference	95% Confidence Interval Lower	Upper
Equal variances assumed	6.353	(.012)	.699	998	.484	.306	−.553	1.165
Equal variances not assumed			(.705)	(992.498)	(.481)	.306	−.546	1.158

Note: The first panel shows characteristics of each group. The second panel provides the test statistic, degrees of freedom, and *p* value.

If we were to reject the null hypothesis, there would be a 48% chance of making a Type I error. Along with the degrees of freedom (b), this nonsignificant result can be confirmed in the *t* table. Therefore, we conclude that there is no significant difference in number of close friends between men and women ($t = 0.71$, $df = 993$, $p = .48$). Said much the same way, any difference between men's and women's number of close friends is likely due to chance.

Example 2: Children and Friends (Directional)

A second example examines whether having children (anykids) is associated with differences in number of close friends (friendstotal). The null hypothesis (H_0) states that there is no difference in the number of close friends between those who do not have children and those who do ($\mu_1 \neq \mu_2$). Since individuals with children might have less time to spend with friends, a directional alternative hypothesis is proposed. This hypothesis states that those without children will have more close friends than those with children ($\mu_1 > \mu_2$).

Table 8.11 provides the results of the t test for statistical significance. The table provides important information about characteristics of the subsamples. You can see that, on average, individuals *with* children (Group 2) have about one fewer close friend than those without children. This provides some preliminary support for the directional alternative hypothesis. Since the coefficient provided for Levene's Test is *not* significant, the assumption for homogeneity of variances has not been violated. As such, the results should be interpreted along the top line that reads "equal variances assumed."

Recall from earlier that when a one-tailed test is employed for a directional hypothesis, the sign of the t statistic is important. In particular, a positive t statistic indicates that Group 1 is larger than Group 2 ($\mu_1 > \mu_2$). The results point to a t statistic of 2.2, which is in line with our directional hypothesis. The p value presented is for a two-tailed test and, therefore, needs to be converted to a p value for a one-tailed test. In order to do so, simply cut the p value in

TABLE 8.11 ● Results of an Independent Samples t Test for the Variables anykids and friendstotal

Group Statistics					
	Has Children or Not	N	Mean	Std. Deviation	Std. Error Mean
Total close friends	No kids	369	8.66	6.534	.340
	Kids	631	7.66	7.099	.283

Independent Samples Test								
	Levene's Test		t Test for Equality of Means					
Dependent Variable: Total Close Friends							95% Confidence Interval of the Difference	
	F	Sig.	t	df	Sig. (2-tailed)	Mean Difference	Lower	Upper
Equal variances assumed	.009	.925	2.221	998	.027	1.004	.117	1.890
Equal variances not assumed			2.269	822.416	.024	1.004	.136	1.872

half. The p value for this one-tailed study is .014, which is below the .05 alpha threshold. This means that we can confidently reject the null hypothesis. Our conclusion is that the mean number of close friends is significantly higher for those who do not have children compared to those who do ($t = 2.22$, $df = 998$, $p < .05$).

The *t*-Test Overview

The independent samples t test is used to test the relationship between a dichotomous independent variable and an interval/ratio dependent variable. Depending on the hypothesis, the test can be either one-tailed or two-tailed. The t statistic (obtained t value) is a numerical representation of the difference between the means for each group—a larger t statistic indicates greater differences. The t statistic and critical value are compared in order to ascertain whether the null hypothesis should be rejected. The next section explores a similar parametric test, analysis of variance, which compares means for nominal variables with *more than two categories*.

One-Way Analysis of Variance

Like the independent samples t test, the **analysis of variance**, referred to as ANOVA, tests for differences in mean scores across independent groups.[9] Unlike t tests, however, ANOVA is capable of testing differences across *more than two groups*.[10] Accordingly, the independent variable is a categorical variable with more than two categories, and the dependent variable is an interval/ratio variable.[11] For example, an ANOVA would be an appropriate test for how number of friends (interval/ratio dependent variable) differs across sexual orientations (nominal independent variable).

ANOVA Assumptions and Notation

As a parametric test, ANOVA has a number of assumptions regarding distribution and variance. Three important assumptions are that (a) the data are normally distributed for each group, (b) the variations are the same across groups, and (c) there are no extreme outliers in any of the groups. One way to check for outliers within groups is to explore modified boxplots separately for each group (see Chapter 5). In the case of the first two assumptions, ANOVA can

---

[9] One-way analysis of variance is also known as single-factor analysis of variance.

[10] Analysis of variance can also be conducted on two groups, but the process is more complicated than the t test (which does the same and produces the same outcome).

[11] There are several other types of ANOVA that are not covered in this chapter. Perhaps the most commonly used is the one-way repeated measures ANOVA, which is used when comparing measures of the dependent variable from the same individuals.

still produce accurate results if the assumptions are not violated too seriously. ANOVA uses sample information to estimate population characteristics across multiple groups. Therefore, there is specific notation to denote population and sample characteristics (see Table 8.12).

ANOVA Hypotheses

The null hypothesis (H_0) in an ANOVA is that there is no significant difference among any of the groups' means ($\mu_1 = \mu_2 = \mu_3 = \ldots \mu_g$). This notation simply states that all populations have the same mean; the letter g represents the total number of groups (i.e., the number of categories in the independent variable). The alternative hypothesis (H_a) is that at least two of the groups are significantly different. Although the groups are likely to differ to some extent, ANOVA tests whether those differences are either so small that they could be attributed to chance, or large enough to be statistically significant. The test does not make any statement about where the differences lie (i.e., between which groups). Additional tests are needed in order to make more specific determinations. Additionally, since we are comparing multiple groups, ANOVA does not accommodate directional hypotheses.

ANOVA Test Statistic and Degrees of Freedom

In ANOVA, differences in means are tested through the *analysis of their variance*. In doing so, we find out how much variance in the dependent variable is due to differences *within* individual groups versus between, or across, the groups. Therefore, in order to obtain the test statistic (the F statistic), it is necessary to compare *variation within* and *variation between* each of the groups. A brief summary of how to obtain the F statistic is outlined in Box 8.1. This

---

TABLE 8.12 ● Standard Statistical Notation Used for Analysis of Variance (ANOVA)

Number of groups			g	
An individual			i	
A group			j	
Grand mean			$\bar{\bar{X}}$	
	Size	**Mean**	**Standard Deviation**	**Variance**
Population	N	μ	σ	σ^2
Groups (g)	n_j	$\bar{X}_j$	s_j	s_j^2

Note: $N = n_1 + n_2 + n_3 \ldots + n_g$.

BOX 8.1:
HOW TO OBTAIN THE F STATISTIC

In analysis of variance, three types of variation are calculated: the total variance, the within-group variance, and the between-group variance. In order to explore this variation, we calculate several means. A **grand mean** is the mean on the dependent variable for the entire sample; the formula for calculating the grand mean is shown in Formula 8.5. Within-group means are means on the dependent variable for each individual group. The formula used to calculate within-group means is shown in Formula 8.6. We use the information on grand and group means to find the sums of squares.

The **total sum of squares** (SST) is the sum of the squared difference of each individual score in the sample from the grand mean. This number represents how individuals in the whole sample vary around the grand mean (see Formula 8.7). The **within-group sum of squares** (SSW) is the squared difference of each individual from his or her individual group's mean. The resulting three numbers are added together to make up the SSW (see Formula 8.8). The **between-group sum of squares** (SSB) is a comparison of the individual group means to the grand mean. The squared difference between the grand mean and the group mean is multiplied by the group *n*. The numbers are summed, and the resulting number is the SSB (see Formula 8.9). One way to cross-check the formula is to make sure that SSB + SSW = SST.

In order to obtain the test statistic, two degrees of freedom are necessary. The **between-group degrees of freedom** are calculated using the formula shown in Formula 8.10. Formula 8.11 is used to calculate the **within-group degrees of freedom**.

The information on sums of squares and degrees of freedom allows us to calculate the between-group mean square and the within-group mean square. The formula for the between-group mean square is to divide the between-group sum of squares by the between-group degrees of freedom, which is shown in Formula 8.12. To find the within-group mean square, you divide the within-group sum of squares by the within-group degrees of freedom (see Formula 8.13). Dividing the between-group mean square by the within-group mean square results in the test statistic for ANOVA, the *F* statistic. Therefore, the **F statistic** is a ratio of the variance between groups to the variance within groups (see Formula 8.14).

Formula 8.5 Grand Mean

$$\bar{\bar{X}} = \frac{\sum_{i=1}^{N} X}{N}$$

Formula 8.6 Group Means

$$\bar{X}_j = \frac{\sum_{i=1}^{N_j} X}{N_j}$$

(Continued)

(Continued)

Formula 8.7 Total Sum of Squares (SST)

$$SST = \sum_{i=1}^{N}\left(X - \bar{X}\right)^2$$

Formula 8.8 Within-Group Sum of Squares (SSW)

$$SSW = \sum_{j=1}^{g}\{\sum_{i=1}^{N_j}\left(X - \bar{X}_j\right)^2\}$$

Formula 8.9 Between-Group Sum of Squares (SSB)

$$SSB = \sum_{j=1}^{g}N_j\left(\bar{X}_j - \bar{X}\right)^2$$

Formula 8.10 Between-Group Degrees of Freedom (df_1)

$$df_1 = g - 1$$

Formula 8.11 Within-Group Degrees of Freedom (df_2)

$$df_2 = N - g$$

Formula 8.12 Between-Group Mean Square (BMS)

$$BMS = BSS/df_1$$

Formula 8.13 Within-Group Mean Square (WMS)

$$WMS = WSS/df_2$$

Formula 8.14 *F* Statistic

$$F = BMS/WMS$$

information is provided because it often helps with interpretation to know how to get from A to Z (or F, as it were). This summary does not include computation; however, formulas are provided to help illustrate the steps in the process of analyzing variance.

The *F* statistic represents *the ratio of the variation between groups and within groups*. A large value of *F* indicates that the variation between groups is larger than the variation within groups. Since the *F* statistic is a ratio, the closer the obtained value is to 1, the smaller the between-group differences. Therefore, the larger the *F* statistic, the greater the difference *between* groups—and the more likely we are to reject the null hypothesis. Figure 8.3 presents two panels that illustrate clearly how the distribution of groups would appear if (a) the variation between groups is much larger than the variation within groups or (b) if the variation within groups is much larger than the variation between groups.

ANOVA Table

F tables are commonly presented separately based on alpha levels—one for an alpha level of .05 and one for an alpha level of .01 (see Appendix D). Each table is organized with between-group degrees of freedom across the columns and the within-group degrees of freedom down the rows. Therefore, in order to locate the appropriate critical value in the table, two values for degrees of freedom are needed. The between-group degrees of freedom are calculated by the number of groups (g) – 1. The within-group degrees of freedom are calculated by the full sample $N - g$ (the number of groups).

As with other tests of statistical significance, the value of the *F* statistic (obtained from the data) is compared to the value of *F* critical (obtained in the table) in order to make a statement about the null hypothesis. If the *F* statistic is higher than the *F* critical (see Appendix D and the small sample in Table 8.13), then the test statistic falls within the region of rejection and we reject the null hypothesis. In that case, we conclude that the group means are not equal—at least two of them differ significantly. On the other hand, if the value of the *F* statistic is lower than the *F* critical value, the test statistic lands in the nonrejection region, and we fail to reject the null hypothesis (see Figure 8.4).

FIGURE 8.3 ● **Separated Curves in Panel (a) and Individual Standalone Curves in Panel (b)**

(a) Variation Between > Variation Within

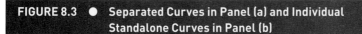

| Group 1 | Group 2 | Group 3 |

(b) Variation Within > Variation Between

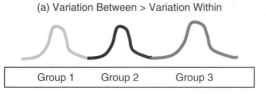

TABLE 8.13 ● A Small Section of the F Table for an Alpha Level of .05

Critical Values of F

Y_2	Y_1 1	2	3	4	5	6	7	8	9	10	11	12	15	20
1	161.4	199.5	215.7	224.6	230.2	234	236.8	238.9	240.5	241.9	243	243.9	245.9	248
2	18.51	19	19.16	19.25	19.3	19.33	19.35	19.37	19.38	19.4	19.4	19.41	19.43	19.45
3	10.13	9.55	9.26	9.12	9.01	8.94	8.89	8.85	8.81	8.79	8.76	8.74	8.7	8.66
4	7.71	6.94	6.59	6.39	6.26	6.16	6.09	6.04	6	5.96	5.94	5.91	5.86	5.8
5	6.61	5.79	5.41	5.19	5.05	4.95	4.88	4.82	4.77	4.74	4.7	4.68	4.62	4.56
6	5.99	5.14	4.76	4.53	4.39	4.28	4.21	4.15	4.1	4.06	4.03	4	3.94	3.87
7	5.59	4.74	4.35	4.12	3.97	3.87	3.79	3.73	3.68	3.64	3.6	3.57	3.51	3.44
8	5.32	4.46	4.07	3.84	3.69	3.58	3.5	3.44	3.39	3.35	3.31	3.28	3.22	3.15
9	5.12	4.26	3.86	3.63	3.48	3.37	3.29	3.23	3.18	3.14	3.1	3.07	3.01	2.94
10	4.96	4.1	3.71	3.48	3.33	3.22	3.14	3.07	3.02	2.98	2.94	2.91	2.85	2.77
11	4.84	3.98	3.59	3.36	3.2	3.09	3.01	2.95	2.9	2.85	2.82	2.79	2.72	2.65

Note: A separate F table provides F critical values for an alpha level of .01.

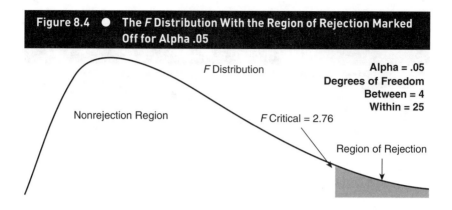

Figure 8.4 ● The *F* Distribution With the Region of Rejection Marked Off for Alpha .05

ANOVA Output and Interpretation

When interpreting and writing up the results of an ANOVA, keep in mind that the results are correlational. As such, it is important to avoid making claims about causal relationships. Additionally, when discussing your results, be sure to include information about the hypothesis, the value of the *F* statistic, between- and within-group degrees of freedom, and the *p* value. The next section analyzes data using ANOVA and includes annotated output to help you interpret the results of your own research. The following examples are based on the analysis of a nonrandom sample of 1,000 U.S. adult men and women.

Example 1: Level of Education and Number of Close Friends

The first example examines differences in the number of friends across different levels of education. The ANOVA uses an ordinal-level independent variable, level of education, which consists of five groups: less than high school, high school, some college, college degree, and postgraduate degree. Although the independent variable is ordinal, the categories are treated as though they are nominal variables—nothing about their order is taken into account. The dependent variable is number of close friends. The null hypothesis (H_0) states that the mean number of close friends is the same across all levels of education. The alternative hypothesis (H_a) is that the mean number of friends differs significantly between at least two of the levels of education. Table 8.14 presents the results of a one-way ANOVA.

The first part of the table provides information on the sample characteristics, including the *n*, mean, and standard deviation for each group. Each of the means presented in the table is the within-group mean. The total mean (at the bottom) is the grand mean. The bottom part of the table provides information on the ANOVA test for statistical significance. The sum of squares and mean square were discussed in Box 8.1. Importantly, the *F* statistic, 2.3, is not

| TABLE 8.14 ● Results of a One-Way Analysis of Variance for the Variables Level of Education (educ) and Total Number of Close Friends (friendstotal) |

| Dependent Variable: Total Number of Close Friends | | | | | |
| | | | | 95% Confidence Interval | |
	N	Mean	Std. Deviation	Std. Error	Lower	Upper
Less than high school	5	15.40	9.839	4.400	3.18	27.62
High school or equivalent	81	6.83	6.924	.769	5.30	8.36
Some college or AA	309	7.82	7.078	.403	7.02	8.61
College degree	322	8.17	7.367	.411	7.36	8.98
Postgraduate degree	283	8.31	6.010	.357	7.61	9.01
Total	1,000	8.03	6.909	.218	7.60	8.46

| ANOVA | | | | | |
| Dependent Variable: Total Number of Close Friends | | | | | |
	Sum of Squares	df	Mean Square	F	Sig.
Between groups	431.709	4	107.927	2.272	.060
Within groups	47261.507	995	47.499		
Total	47693.216	999			

Note: The first panel of this table provides descriptive statistics for each level of education. The second panel provides information about the test statistic, degrees of freedom, and *p* value.

significant at the .05 level. Therefore, we fail to reject the null hypothesis. We conclude that there is no significant difference in the number of friends across each of the different levels of education ($F = 2.3$; $df_{between} = 4$, $df_{within} = 995$; $p = .06$).

Example 2: Age Group and Number of Close Friends

The next example uses the same dependent variable but examines difference in mean number of close friends across three different age categories. Again, age category (`agegroup`) is an ordinal variable, created from an interval/ratio variable—but the order is not taken into account. There are three categories for the independent variable: young adults (age 18–34), midlife adults (age 35–64), and older adults (65+). The null hypothesis (H_0) states that the mean number of close friends is the same across all three groups. The alternative hypothesis (H_a) is that the mean number of friends differs between at least two of the age groups. Table 8.15 provides the results from an ANOVA test of statistical significance for this hypothesis.

The first part of the table shows sample characteristics, including the n for each group in the sample, the within-group means, and the grand mean. The second part provides information about the hypothesis test. The F statistic, 11.2, is larger than 1, suggesting that there might be more between-group than within-group variance. Moreover, the level of significance is .001, indicating that we reject the null hypothesis. We conclude that at least two of the age groups differ significantly in their number of close friends ($F = 11.2$; $df_{between} = 2$,

TABLE 8.15 ● Results of a One-Way Analysis of Variance for the Variables Age Group (agegroup) and Total Number of Close Friends (friendstotal)

Dependent Variable: Total Number of Close Friends						
	N	Mean	Std. Deviation	Std. Error	95% Confidence Interval for Mean Lower	Upper
Early adulthood (18–34)	313	9.50	7.070	.400	8.72	10.29
Adulthood (35–64)	635	7.28	6.754	.268	6.75	7.80
Older adulthood (65+)	52	8.33	6.465	.896	6.53	10.13
Total	1,000	8.03	6.909	.218	7.60	8.46

ANOVA					
recode: collapsed midpoint maximum total friends					
	Sum of Squares	df	Mean Square	F	Sig.
Between groups	1,046.759	2	523.380	11.186	.000
Within groups	46,646.457	997	46.787		
Total	47,693.216	999			

Note: The first panel of this table provides descriptive statistics for each age group. The second panel provides information about the test statistic, degrees of freedom, and *p* value.

$df_{within} = 997; p < .001$). However, based on these results alone, we are unable to determine which groups are significantly different. Post hoc analyses are necessary in order to make this determination.

Post Hoc Analysis

As mentioned earlier, ANOVA does not indicate *which* pairs of groups are significantly different—it could be all pairs of groups or it could be a single pair. Therefore, in the event that you reject the null hypothesis, there are several additional procedures, called **post hoc tests**, that can help you tease out the effects of individual pairs. One common approach is to conduct multiple independent sample *t* tests to examine paired differences. While this might be useful to get a rough estimate of paired differences, there are at least two reasons this is a problematic approach. First, a series of paired *t* tests is computationally inefficient (e.g., an independent variable with only four categories would require six individual *t* tests). Second, and more important, conducting multiple tests increases the likelihood of making a Type I error. There are a number of post hoc procedures that researchers can use to explore paired differences; however, they are not covered in this text.

ANOVA Overview

Analysis of variance is a test of statistical significance that allows a researcher to examine mean differences across multiple groups. The *F* statistic is the ratio of the variation between groups and the variation within groups. If a researcher rejects the null hypothesis, he concludes that there are significant differences between at least two of the groups' means. However, ANOVA does not determine which means. Post hoc analyses are needed in order to tease out these paired effects.

Conclusion

Hypotheses are testable statements about the relationship between variables. Additionally, tests of statistical significance allow researchers to test hypotheses and draw inferences about larger populations. When making inferences about a larger population, the first steps are to (a) establish null and alternative hypotheses, including—if applicable—choosing whether the alternative hypothesis is directional; (b) choose the appropriate statistical analysis and calculate a test statistic; and (c) make a determination about the null hypothesis based on the test statistic, degrees of freedom, and *p* value in the study.

In order to avoid poor interpretation or misrepresentation of your results, it is important to remember several important points about hypothesis testing. First, adequate information about your sample characteristics, hypotheses, and alpha levels must be provided to support your claims. This transparency is necessary in order for scientific research to remain rigorous. Second, avoid using causal language when tests are not designed to test for causality. The tests of statistical significance discussed in this chapter were designed to test for relationships (i.e., correlations) between variables. It would be misleading to suggest, for example, that not having children *causes* individuals to have fewer friends since the *t* test only showed a *correlation* between the two variables. Third, it is important not to conflate the idea of statistical significance with theoretical or practical importance. Since tests of statistical significance are influenced by sample sizes, it is equally important to focus on statistical power and effect size in the interpretation of your results. These concepts are discussed further in Chapter 10.

Terms

alpha 116

alternative hypothesis (H_a) 114

analysis of variance (ANOVA) 135

between-group degrees of
    freedom 137

between-group sum of squares 137

chi-square distribution 122

chi-square test of
    independence 119

chi-square critical value 122

critical value 122

degrees of freedom 122

difference between means 129

directional alternative
    hypothesis 114

expected frequencies 120

fail to reject the null
    hypothesis 114

F statistic 137

grand mean 137

homogeneity of variance 128

independent 120

independent samples *t* test 127

nondirectional alternative
    hypothesis 114

nonparametric tests 119

nonrejection region 117

null hypothesis (H_0) 113

observed frequencies 120

obtained *t* statistic 129

obtained value 121

one-tailed test 118

parametric tests 119

post hoc tests 144

p value 116

region of rejection 117

reject the null hypothesis 114

statistically significant 116

t critical values 131

t distribution 131

test statistic 117

total sum of squares 137

two-tailed test 118

Type I error 115

Type II error 115

within-group degrees of
    freedom 137

within-group sum of squares 137

9

How to Measure the Relationship Between Nominal and Ordinal Variables

Choosing the Correct Measure of Association

As we discuss here, choosing the appropriate measure of association depends, first, on the level of measurement used for the independent and dependent variables being analyzed. You will need to know whether the variables you are using are nominal, dichotomous nominal, or ordinal. For further explanation, please read ahead.

Trying to Reduce Error (PRE Statistics)

Proportional reduction in error (PRE) statistics allow us to determine the proportional reduction of error achieved by adding one or more variables to an analysis (even if it is the initial independent variable).

"PRE measures are derived by comparing the errors made in predicting the dependent variable while ignoring the independent variable with errors made when making predictions that use information about the independent variable" (Frankfort-Nachmias & Leon-Guerrero, 2009, p. 386). There are many PRE statistics available from which to choose. Some are favored in particular disciplines over others, and some are used with data that exhibit particular distributions or characteristics. We cover four of the most commonly used PRE statistics in this chapter: lambda, gamma, Somer's *d*, and Kendall's tau-*b*.

For nominal variables, a PRE statistic that we can use is lambda. For details on how lambda is specifically calculated, see Chapter 12 of *Social Statistics for a Diverse Society* (Frankfort-Nachmias & Leon-Guerrero, 2009) or Chapter 13 of *Adventures in Social Research* (Babbie, Wagner, & Zaino, 2015).

Calculating and Interpreting Lambda

Lambda is a measure of association for nominal variables. It ranges from 0 to 1. When lambda equals zero, there is no association at all; none of the variation in the dependent variable can be explained by the variation in the independent variable. When lambda equals 1, there is a perfect (deterministic) association;

TABLE 9.1 ● Lambda in SPSS Statistics Output

Directional Measures			Value	Asymptotic Standardized Error[a]	Approximate T[b]	Approximate Significance
Nominal by Nominal	Lambda	Symmetric	.023	.011	2.033	.042
		FAVOR OR OPPOSE DEATH PENALTY FOR MURDER Dependent	.045	.022	2.033	.042
		RACE OF RESPONDENT Dependent	.000	.000	.[c]	.[c]
	Goodman and Kruskal tau	FAVOR OR OPPOSE DEATH PENALTY FOR MURDER Dependent	.046	.009		.000[d]
		RACE OF RESPONDENT Dependent	.025	.005		.000[d]

[a] Not assuming the null hypothesis.

[b] Using the asymptotic standard error assuming the null hypothesis.

[c] Cannot be computed because the asymptotic standard error equals zero.

[d] Based on chi-square approximation.

100% (all) of the variation in the dependent variable can be explained by the variation of the independent variable.

To compute lambda by hand, we would calculate E_1 and E_2. E_1 represents the number of errors that would be made predicting the dependent variable while ignoring the information available from the independent variable. E_2 signifies the errors of prediction of the dependent variable while taking into account the information that has been obtained from the independent variable. Using those error terms, lambda is calculated as follows:

$$\lambda = \frac{E_1 - E_2}{E_1}$$

Typically, lambda is presented as an asymmetrical measure of association; this is the case in *Social Statistics for a Diverse Society* (Frankfort-Nachmias & Leon-Guerrero, 2009) as well as in *Adventures in Social Research* (Babbie et al., 2018).

In Table 9.1, the value of lambda to be used can be found in the "Value" column in the row indicating the correct dependent variable. Since lambda is asymmetrical, it is important to choose the correct dependent variable. In this case, "cappun" (favor or oppose the death penalty for murder) is the appropriate dependent variable. We see that the value of lambda is very small at 0.045; however, it is statistically significant ($p = .042$). The p value refers to the probability that the result is due to chance; a smaller number for p ($p = .05$ or less) is an indication of statistical significance.

Calculating and Interpreting Gamma

Gamma (γ), Kendall's tau-*b*, and Somers' *d* are all measures of association for ordinal and dichotomous nominal variables. All three of these PRE statistics can take on values ranging from -1 to $+1$. A value of $+1$ indicates that there is a deterministic and positive association such that 100% of the variation in the dependent variable is explained by the variation in the independent variable. By contrast, a value of -1 indicates, again, that there is a deterministic association, but that it is negative association. Although all of the variation in the dependent variable is accounted for by the variation in the independent variable, the association is in the opposite (negative) direction. When gamma, Kendall's tau-*b*, or Somers' *d* is equal to zero, this is an indication that there is no association between the variables whatsoever; none of the variation in the dependent variable can be accounted for by the variation in the independent variable. It is extremely rare to find a PRE statistic equal to either $+1$, -1, or 0. Those are the most extreme cases. Knowing what happens in those extreme cases is useful for interpretation of the actual values. Of course, the closer the value of any of these measures is to zero, the weaker the association. The closer the value is to either $+1$ or -1, the stronger the association, in the respective direction.

Each of these PRE measures is calculated using the concept of pairs. If all possible dyads were selected from a dataset and we looked at how each value in the pair "scored" on each of two variables, we could see whether they both score higher on one than the other or whether one scores higher on one variable and lower on the other. In the former case, the pairs are called *same-order pairs* and denoted *Ns*, whereas pairs in the latter case are labeled *inverse-ordered pairs* and denoted *Nd*. We could also see if the two values in each pair have the same score on one or both variables (independent variable *X* or dependent variable *Y*). Those with equal values (tied) on the independent variables are represented by *Tx*, whereas those tied on the dependent variable are marked with *Ty*.

Gamma (γ), sometimes referred to as Goodman and Kruskal's gamma, is a symmetrical measure of association that is calculated as follows:

$$\gamma = \frac{Ns - Nd}{Ns + Nd}$$

In General

In Table 9.2, note the value for gamma: 0.374. It, too, is statistically significant ($p = .000$). When $\gamma = 0.374$, we can say that 37.4% of the variation in the dependent variable can be explained by the variation in the independent variable. It is important to determine which measure best suits the variables being researched so that the appropriate proportion of reduction in error can be computed (Wagner, 2016).

For This Specific Example

The data used for the above example come from the General Social Survey, described earlier in Chapter 1. The two variables used for the analysis are satjob and satfin. Satfin is the variable representing how satisfied the

TABLE 9.2 ● Gamma and Kendall's Tau-*b* in SPSS Statistics Output

Symmetric Measures				
	Value	Asymptotic Standardized Error[a]	Approximate T[b]	Approximate Significance
Ordinal by Kendall's tau-*b*	.237	.020	11.678	.000
Ordinal Gamma	.374	.030	11.678	.000
N of Valid Cases	1892			

[a] Not assuming the null hypothesis.
[b] Using the asymptotic standard error assuming the null hypothesis.

respondent was with his or her financial situation. `Satjob` reveals the level of satisfaction that the respondent feels about his or her job or housework. Since gamma is symmetrical, it doesn't make any difference which variable is considered as the independent variable and which is considered as the dependent variable. However, let's choose `satjob` as the predictor or independent variable, since most people earn the lion's share of their income through a primary job, and it stands to reason that the job is more likely to play a role in satisfaction with finances than finances are to play in the role of satisfaction with one's job.* Given that the value of gamma is equal to 0.374, we can say that 37.4% of the variation in satisfaction with one's finances can be explained by the variation in one's satisfaction with one's job.

Calculating and Interpreting Somers' *d*

Somers' *d* is an asymmetrical measure of association; SPSS Statistics uses the term *directional measure* to describe asymmetrical measures. Somers' *d* is calculated using paired observations, as follows:

$$d = \frac{Ns - Nd}{Ns + Nd + Ty}$$

In General

In Table 9.3, locate the value for Somers' *d* that is appropriate for your analysis; that is, determine which variable will be the independent and which will be the dependent variable. Here, the values are .244 and .230. If your independent variable and dependent variable are such that you will use .244, then this would be interpreted as 24.4% of the variation in the dependent variable is accounted for by the variation in the independent variable. Similarly, if your independent variable and dependent variable are such that you will use .230, then this value would be interpreted as 23% of the variation in the dependent variable can be explained by the variation in the independent variable.

For This Specific Example

In Table 9.3, the value for Somers' *d* is located in the "Value" column in the row with the appropriate variable listed as the dependent variable. Note that, like lambda, Somers' *d* is asymmetrical; therefore, the two values given, where the dependent variables are different, will be different. Somers' *d* is statistically significant in this case ($p = .000$) regardless of which variable

---

*Of course, there are other theories that you might wish to test, including but not limited to an examination of how much of a role income from one's job contributes to satisfaction with one's job. In other words, it might be a worthy endeavor to determine the relative effects that income and other factors have on career satisfaction.

TABLE 9.3 ● Somers' *d* in SPSS Statistics Output						
Directional Measures						
			Value	Asymptotic Standar- dized Error[a]	Approxi- mate T[b]	Approxi- mate Signifi- cance
Ordinal by Ordinal	Somers' *d*	Symmetric	.237	.020	11.678	.000
		SATISFACTION WITH FINANCIAL SITUATION Dependent	.244	.021	11.678	.000
		JOB OR HOUSEWORK Dependent	.230	.020	11.678	.000

[a] Not assuming the null hypothesis.
[b] Using the asymptotic standard error assuming the null hypothesis.

is treated as the dependent variable. Its value is 0.244 with `satfin` treated as the dependent variable. We can interpret this by saying that 24.4% of the variation in satisfaction with financial situation can be explained by the variation in satisfaction with job or housework. Somers' *d* would be 0.230 with `satjob` as the dependent variable. This tells us that 23% of the variation in job satisfaction can be accounted for by the variation in satisfaction with financial situation. In either of these cases, the errors of prediction have reduced by almost one quarter with the introduction of an independent variable (Wagner, 2016).

Calculating and Interpreting Kendall's Tau-*b*

Kendall's tau-*b* is also a symmetrical measure of association. The following equation shows how Kendall's tau-*b* is calculated using pairs:

$$\text{tau-}b = \frac{Ns - Nd}{\sqrt{(Ns + Nd + Tx)(Ns + Nd + Ty)}}$$

In General

In Table 9.4, Kendall's tau-*b* is given as 0.237. Note that it is also statistically significant, with $p = 0.000$. When Kendall's tau-*b* = 0.237, we are able to say that 23.7% of the variation in the dependent variable can be explained by the variation in the independent variable (Wagner, 2016).

TABLE 9.4 ● Gamma and Kendall's Tau-*b* in SPSS Statistics Output				
Symmetric Measures				
	Value	**Asymptotic Standardized Error[a]**	**Approximate T[b]**	**Approximate Significance**
Ordinal by Kendall's tau-*b*	.237	.020	11.678	.000
Ordinal Gamma	.374	.030	11.678	.000
N of Valid Cases	1892			

[a] Not assuming the null hypothesis.
[b] Using the asymptotic standard error assuming the null hypothesis.

For This Specific Example

As before, the two variables used for the analysis are `satjob` and `satfin`. `Satfin` is the variable representing how satisfied the respondent was with his or her financial situation. `Satjob` reveals the level of satisfaction that the respondent feels about his or her job or housework. Since Kendall's tau-*b* is symmetrical, it doesn't make any difference which variable is considered as the independent variable and which variable is considered as the dependent variable. Let's choose `satjob` as the predictor or independent variable. Given that the value of Kendall's tau-*b* is equal to .237, we can say that 23.7% of the variation in satisfaction with one's finances can be explained by the variation in one's satisfaction with one's job.

Interpreting PRE Statistics Overview

In general, there is a recipe for interpreting PRE statistics. This is a recipe to follow just as if you were baking a cheesecake. Follow the directions, and you will either have a delicious cheesecake or an insightful statistical interpretation. This also extends to r^2, a PRE statistic for interval-ratio variables that is covered in Chapter 11.

<<PRE value times 100>>% of the variation in <<dependent variable>> can be accounted for by the variation in <<independent variable>>.

If there is more than one independent variable involved in the PRE statistic calculation, then the interpretation can be adjusted to include the extra variable(s):

<<PRE value times 100>>% of the variation in <<dependent variable>> can be accounted for by the variation in <<independent variable #1>> and the variation in <<independent variable #2>>.

You can add as many variables at the end of the sentence as necessary, determined by the number of independent variables that are used in your prediction analysis of the dependent variable.

Multivariate Analysis With PRE Statistics for Nominal and Ordinal Variables

So far in this chapter, we have covered the role of PRE statistics for bivariate analyses and, in particular, have focused on four such measures: lambda, gamma, Somers' *d*, and Kendall's tau-*b*. Proportional reduction of error statistics are not limited exclusively to bivariate situations. The very same calculation, ranges, and interpretations apply for multivariate analysis using PRE measures for nominal and ordinal variables.

When incorporating a third variable, typically the results will be split, as in separate crosstabulation tables. Suppose you are analyzing General Social Survey data and are interested in adding a variable, sex, categorized by male and nonmale. In addition to a "final" crosstab showing the independent and dependent variables you started with (whether respondent's satisfaction with job and respondent's satisfaction with financial situation, as stated previously, or another pair of variables), you will also have a crosstab for male and another crosstab for nonmale. For each one of those tables (total, male, nonmale), there will be a PRE statistic. Suppose you've decide to use gamma. You will have three gammas to examine and interpret.

First, which of the three, if any, are statistically significant? Below, you'll find the likely possibilities and what that indicates.

	Total	Male	Nonmale
(a)	significant	significant	significant
(b)	significant	significant	not significant
(c)	significant	not significant	significant
(d)	significant	not significant	not significant
(e)	not significant	significant	not significant
(f)	not significant	not significant	significant
(g)	not significant	not significant	not significant

With case (a), this is an indication that the relationship is statistically significant overall and statistically significant for each of the subgroups enumerated from the categories of the third variable entered into your analysis, in this case, sex.

The next possibility (b) presents a case where the relationship is statistically significant for males, but not for nonmales. In this case, the statistical significance in males was strong enough, through magnitude and/or sample size, to carry the statistical significance for the entire sample.

In case (c), this is the same as with case (b), except that the nonmale subgroup was significant and was strong enough, through magnitude and/or sample size, to carry the statistical significance for the whole sample.

Case (d) provides an interesting situation, where the overall sample is statistically significant, but neither subgroup is statistically significant. By introducing the third variable in this case, the initial relationship is brought into question, perhaps caused by some nonrandom feature of the demographics when examined collectively. For instance, there may be no relationship between shoe size and height for women and no relationship between shoe size and height for men, but when examining the group composed of both men and women, it may appear that there is a relationship since the two nonrelated data groups themselves may appear to form a pattern.

With case (e), the overall relationship was not statistically significant, but one of the subgroups created by the categories of the third variable (male) was statistically significant, though the other subgroup, nonmale, was not statistically significant. The statistical significance for the male subgroup was of insufficient magnitude and/or sample size to carry the statistical significance for the entire sample.

Likewise with case (f), the overall relationship was not statistically significant, but one of the subgroups created by the categories of the third variable (nonmale) was statistically significant, while the male group was not significant. Here, the nonmale group's statistical significance was not of a great enough magnitude and/or sample size to carry significance for the whole sample.

With case (g), we have a relatively straightforward situation where the overall relationship is not statistically significant and neither of the subgroups exhibits a statistically significant relationship.

After discussion of the statistical significance of the categories of the third variable, you can then illustrate the pattern of the relationship, if any, by use of the computed value of the PRE statistic, whether it be gamma or any other. Here, you can note the comparative PRE to determine in which category or categories of the third variable the prediction of the dependent variable from the independent is strongest. You can revisit the recipes for interpreting PRE statistics contained in the Interpreting PRE Statistics Overview section.

Terms

gamma 150	proportional reduction in error
Kendall's tau-*b* 152	(PRE) statistics 147
lambda 148	Somers' *d* 151

References

Babbie, E., Wagner, W. E., III, & Zaino, J. (2018). *Adventures in social research: Data analysis using IBM® SPSS® Statistics* (10th ed.). Thousand Oaks, CA: Sage.

Frankfort-Nachmias, C., & Leon-Guerrero, A. (2009). *Social statistics for a diverse society* (5th ed.). Thousand Oaks, CA: Sage.

Wagner, W. (2016). *Using IBM® SPSS® Statistics for research methods and social science statistics* (6th ed.). Thousand Oaks, CA: Sage.

Effect Size

As Chapter 8 discussed, the probability of making a Type I error (a false positive) is represented by alpha (α). A Type II error occurs when a researcher fails to reject the null hypothesis but the null hypothesis is true. The probability of making this type of error is represented by beta (β). Since the probability of making a Type I error is contingent upon *rejecting* the null hypothesis and the probability of making a Type II error is contingent upon *failing to reject* the null hypothesis, the two errors cannot be present at the same time. In fact, the reduction of one type of error makes a study more vulnerable to the other type of error.

If, for example, a researcher wants to set her alpha at .001 in order to be cautious against making a Type I error, she might be erroneous in failing to reject the null hypothesis because of the strict criteria on the *p* level. At the same time, however, relaxing the criteria for rejecting the null hypothesis by setting a higher alpha level, such as .10, to *reduce* the probability of Type II error would, in turn, increase the likelihood of making a Type I error. Researchers try to balance these errors in order to determine whether their results are pointing to *actual* relationships.

Before a study begins, researchers can make determinations about characteristics of the study that need to be present in order to detect effects if they exist. **Statistical power** is an indication of the ability of a test to produce an accurate result if a researcher rejects the null hypothesis. This power helps researchers address questions about whether a given sample size could lead to an effective rejection of the null hypothesis. **A priori power analysis** helps determine the statistical power needed in order to detect relationships in the data. This information is based on the desired sample size, level of alpha, and effect size. Researchers use this information at the outset to avoid conducting studies with either too few or too many participants.

Since the probability of making a Type I error (p value) is largely dependent on the number of individuals in a study, the results of a study will vary based on the sample size. A small sample size can lead to the oversight of meaningful relationships because there are too few data points to detect an effect. On the other hand, a very large sample could produce significant results for even trivial relationships. For this reason, researchers should interpret their findings in light of both statistical significance and effect size. A priori analyses of statistical power and effect size (those that occur before a study begins) are not covered in this book. The remainder of this chapter discusses post hoc measures of effect size. These measures are based on statistical procedures that allow researchers to make determinations about the size of an effect (or relationship) in *practical* terms after they have collected the data for their study.

Effect Size

With the hypothesis tests in Chapter 8, we established whether or not relationships between variables were statistically significant—or whether the effect could be due to chance. However, in order to accurately interpret the findings of a study, researchers must also understand the *magnitude of the effect*. **Effect sizes** help researchers determine whether their results are *meaningful*. While statistical significance tells us how precise we are in our interpretation of an effect, effect size adds the magnitude of that effect. Both are necessary in order to accurately interpret the results of scientific research.

As noted earlier, sample size can make even a trivial effect significant—and statistical significance does not imply that a result is important in practical application. In fact, research results can be statistically significant but substantively trivial. At the same time, results can be nonsignificant but have some substantive value. A nonsignificant relationship simply suggests that findings could have occurred due to chance. In many cases, more data might help move the results toward a more definitive conclusion. On the other hand, analysis on a very large sample will indicate that even miniscule effects are statistically significant. Thus, tests of statistical significance tell us only about the probability that these differences might be *due to chance*; however, the magnitude, or overall relevance, of the relationship is established with effect size.

There are many different varieties of effect size, and the most appropriate measures depend on the data and variables under study. The remainder of this chapter explores common effect size measures that correspond to the tests of statistical significance and association discussed in Chapter 8.

Choosing an Effect Size

As with choosing a test of statistical significance, the most appropriate measure of effect size for a given relationship depends on characteristics of the data and variables under study. Table 10.1 highlights the most common effect size

TABLE 10.1 ●	Common Effect Size Measures for the Tests of Statistical Significance Discussed in Chapter 8
Test Statistic	**Effect Size Measure**
Chi-square (χ^2)	Phi (ϕ) for 2 × 2 and Cramér's V
Independent samples t test	Cohen's d
One-way analysis of variance	Eta squared (η^2)

measures for the statistical procedures introduced in Chapter 8. Each of these is discussed with regard to its use and interpretation.

Effect Sizes for Chi-Square: ϕ and Cramér's V

The **phi coefficient of effect size** (ϕ) for the chi-square test of independence when both variables are dichotomous. Therefore, when conducting a chi-square analysis with a 2 × 2 crosstab, the phi coefficient will indicate the magnitude of difference between the observed and expected frequencies. The coefficient for phi is calculated with the formula shown in Formula 10.1. The resulting coefficient is between 0 and 1. Table 10.2 presents Cohen's (1988) guidelines for interpreting phi.

Formula 10.1 Two Formulas for Effect Size With Chi-Square: (a) Phi (ϕ) and (b) Cramér's V

(a) $\quad \varphi = \sqrt{\dfrac{\chi^2}{N}}$

(b) $\quad V = \sqrt{\dfrac{\dfrac{\chi^2}{n}}{\min(r-1),(c-1)}}$

The value in the denominator is the smaller value between $r - 1$ and $c - 1$.

Taking the example from Chapter 8, a chi-square test of independence tested whether gender is associated with feeling that household chores are an important source of stress (chorestress). The null hypothesis is that gender and chorestress are independent (i.e., not associated). The information presented in the statistical output led us to *reject the null hypothesis*. The results suggested that there was a statistically significant relationship between gender and reporting that chores are an important source of stress ($\chi^2 = 28.3$, $df = 1$, $p < .001$).

Now that we know there is a statistically significant relationship between the two variables, we want to determine whether the relationship is a meaningful one. Since both variables are dichotomous, we can assess the magnitude of the relationship with the phi coefficient of effect size. In this example, the value of ϕ is .17 (Table 10.3). Based on Cohen's guideline for assessing the magnitude of the relationship (Table 10.2), we would conclude that there is a small to medium relationship between gender and chorestress. Therefore, despite

TABLE 10.2 ● Cohen's (1988) Suggested Interpretation of Phi (φ) and Cramér's V Coefficients

Value of φ or Cramér's V	Suggested Interpretation
0.00 through 0.10	Weak/small effect
0.11 through 0.30	Moderate/medium effect
0.31+	Strong/large effect

TABLE 10.3 ● Chi-Square Test of Independence and Effect Size (φ) Between sex and chorestress

	Value	df	Asymp. Sig. (2-sided)
Pearson chi-square	28.288	1	.000
N of valid cases	1000		

Symmetric Measures		
	Value	Approx. Sig.
Phi	.168	.000

TABLE 10.4 ● Chi-Square Test of Independence and Effect Size (Cramér's V) to Test the Relationship Between agegroup and chorestress

Chi-Square Tests			
	Value	df	Asymp. Sig. (2-sided)
Pearson chi-square	13.244	2	.001
Likelihood ratio	14.693	2	.001
Linear-by-linear association	12.423	1	.000
N of valid cases	1,000		

Note: Zero cells (0.0%) have expected count less than 5. The minimum expected count is 11.86.

Symmetric Measures		
	Value	Approx. Sig.
Cramer's V	.115	.001
N of valid cases	1,000	

being a statistically significant relationship (i.e., we have confidence that the relationship is real), the effect is not a particularly large one.

For tables with more than two groups on one or both variables (i.e., non-dichotomous categorical variables), **Cramér's V** provides a measure of effect size with similar guidelines for interpretation (see Table 10.2). Examining the results of a chi-square test of independence between age group (young adult, midlife adult, and older adult) and chorestress would result in a 3 × 2 crosstab. Therefore, Cramér's V would be the appropriate effect size measure to present. Table 10.4 presents the outcome of such an analysis. The results indicate that there is a statistically significant relationship between age group and reporting that chores are an important source of stress ($\chi^2 = 13.2$, $df = 2$, $p < .001$). The effect size, Cramér's V (.12), indicates that while the result of the analysis is statistically significant, the effect is still rather small.

Effect Size for *t* Test: Cohen's *d*

A common effect size provided for a t test is **Cohen's d**, which is equal to the number of standard deviations of difference between the two groups being studied. Therefore, this coefficient is straightforward—it is calculated using the formula shown in Formula 10.2. To facilitate interpretation, Table 10.5 presents Cohen's criteria for assessing the magnitude of the relationship based on effect size d.

Formula 10.2

$$d = \frac{t^2}{\sqrt{df}}$$

Drawing on the same example from Chapter 8 (see Table 10.6), we tested whether or not there was a significant difference in the number of close friends between those who have children and those who do not. The null hypothesis was that the mean number of friends was the same for both groups. The results led us to reject the null hypothesis and conclude that the mean number of close friends was significantly higher for those who do not have children compared to those who do ($t = 2.22$, $df = 998$, $p < .01$). While this is an important finding, it does not tell us *how different* the two groups were. Cohen's d can be calculated using Formula 10.2 and is sometimes provided as an option in statistical analysis applications.[1] In this example, Cohen's d, the effect size for a t test for independent samples, has a value of .16. Therefore, based on Cohen's suggested cutoff points, we would conclude that, despite being a statistically significant difference, there is only a small difference in number of friends for those who have children and those who do not. Variations on Cohen's d, such as **Glass's delta** and **Hedge's g**, provide adjustment for violations in the assumptions of the test.

---

[1] This calculation and interpretation applies only to the independent samples *t* test.

TABLE 10.5 ● Cohen's (1988) Suggested Interpretation for the Value of Cohen's *d*	
Value of Cohen's *d*	**Suggested Interpretation**
0.2	Weak effect
0.5	Moderate effect
0.8	Strong effect

TABLE 10.6 ● Results of an Independent Samples *t* Test for the Dependent Variable friendstotal Between Groups of anykids, With Additional Information on Cohen's *d*

Dependent Variable: Number of Close Friends	t-test for Equality of Means		
	t	*df*	Sig. (2-tailed)
	2.221	998	.027

	Value
Cohen's *d*	0.156
N of valid cases	1,000

Effect Size for One-Way ANOVA: η^2

Eta squared (η^2) is an effect size coefficient to determine the strength of mean differences across multiple groups. This number provides an indication of the amount of variation in the dependent variable that can be explained—or accounted for—by the independent variable. In other words, this effect size measure tells us how much the difference between group means affects the grand mean. The formula to calculate η^2 is shown in Formula 10.3. Additionally, Cohen's guidelines for interpretation are presented in Table 10.7.

Formula 10.3

$$\eta^2 = \frac{SSB}{SST}$$

In the example from Chapter 8 (Table 10.8), we used one-way ANOVA to test whether or not the mean number of close friends was different across three age groups (young adult, midlife adult, and older adult). The null hypothesis was that the mean number of close friends was the same for all three groups. The results led us to reject the null hypothesis. We concluded that at least two of the age groups differed significantly in their number of close friends ($F = 11.2$; $df_{between} = 2$, $df_{within} = 997$; $p < .001$). Again, this finding tells us that we can be confident that at least two of the means significantly differ; however, we do not know the magnitude of these differences.

TABLE 10.7 ● **Cohen's (1988) Guidelines for Interpreting the Value of η^2**

Value of η^2	Suggested Interpretation
0.01	Small effect
0.06	Medium effect
0.14	Large effect

TABLE 10.8 ● **Results of a One-Way Analysis of Variance for the Dependent Variable friendstotal Across Three Different Age Groups (agegroup)**

ANOVA						
Dependent Variable: Total Number of Close Friends						
	Sum of Squares	df	Mean Square	F	Sig.
Between groups	1046.759	2	523.380	11.186	.000
Within groups	46646.457	997	46.787		
Total	47693.216	999			

	Value
Eta squared	0.022
N of valid cases	1,000

Note: Effect size information is presented in the second panel (η^2).

Using Formula 10.3 (or statistical analysis software), we see that the value of η^2 is .02. Therefore, despite being a statistically significant result, the effect size (η^2) indicates that the magnitude of the relationship is small. The mean differences are of little practical importance. Additional effect size measures, such as **omega squared (ω^2)** and **epsilon squared (ε^2)**, correct for sample size differences and the number of categories in the independent variable. There are additional effect size measures, such as the **coefficient of determination (r^2)**, that researchers calculate when examining the magnitude of the relationship between two continuous variables. However, these measures are based on the correlation coefficient, which is discussed in Chapter 11. These effect sizes are discussed in that chapter.

Conclusion

Ellis (2010, pp. 35–42) provides a useful mnemonic to keep in mind when interpreting effect size. He identifies the "three C's of interpretation—context, contribution, and Cohen." First, even small effect sizes can hold some meaning based on their context. In other words, small effects can be meaningful if they (a) lead to important consequences, (b) increase the probability of important consequences, (c) accumulate to lead to larger consequences, and (d) change the way we think about relationships and effects. Second, researchers should keep in mind what a given effect size reveals in the context of previous research findings. Understanding the magnitude and direction of an effect allows researchers to assess the value of their contribution to research on a given topic. Third, Cohen's criteria, discussed in each of the previous sections, provide a useful set of cutoffs for interpretation. However, it is important to remember that these cutoffs are merely *guidelines*. The practical importance of a relationship should also be judged based on the context of the findings and their potential contribution to the literature.

There is a trade-off between the probability of making a Type I error versus a Type II error. Researchers try to minimize these errors by setting an appropriate alpha and conducting studies with sample sizes amenable to finding differences if they exist. The magnitude of an effect—the effect size—provides the context for interpreting whether or not a given research finding is valuable in practical terms. Accordingly, effect size is among the most important elements of statistical interpretation. Statistical significance and effect size give you information on the meaning of your results in two ways. First, you can establish how likely it is that the relationship is a real one (statistical significance). Second, you can establish whether the result is a meaningful one (effect size).

Terms

a priori power analysis 157

coefficient of determination (r^2) 163

Cohen's d 161

Cramér's V 161

effect size 158

epsilon squared (ε^2) 163

eta squared (η^2) 162

Glass's delta 161

Hedge's g 161

omega squared (ω^2) 163

phi coefficient of effect size 159

statistical power 157

References

Cohen, J. (1988). *Statistical power analysis for the behavioral sciences*. Hillsdale, NJ: Lawrence Erlbaum.

Ellis, P. D. (2010). *The essential guide to effect sizes: An introduction to statistical power, meta-analysis and the interpretation of research results*. New York, NY: Cambridge University Press.

How to Interpret and Report Regression Results

What Is a Regression?

In this context, it has nothing to do with a psychiatrist making you stare at a swinging pendulum to get you to go back in your mind to relive memories to discover something about your behavior (though you might see that type of "regression" more in the movies or on television!).

Regression is a statistical tool that allows you to estimate/predict outcomes for interval and ratio (scale, continuous) variables. There are many types of regression, but generally when you hear just the word *regression* in a context of statistics, it means Ordinary Least Squares (OLS) regression. OLS refers to the method that the regression uses to predict or estimate outcomes. **OLS regression** indicates that the sum of all of the squared distances from each observed data point to the prediction line have been minimized. Since the prediction equation will result in a straight line when graphed on a Cartesian plane (*x-y* coordinate axis), this type of analysis is sometimes also called linear regression.

Bivariate regression refers to an OLS regression for two variables: one independent variable (the predictor) and one dependent variable (the variable you wish to predict). **Multivariate regression** (also known as multiple regression) involves two or more independent variables (predictors) and one dependent variable.

Correlation

In order to determine if two variables vary together, you can determine if there is a correlation. To find this correlation, the appropriate statistic to use is **Pearson's *r*** (also known as the **correlation coefficient**).

The range of Pearson's *r* is from –1 to +1. When *r* is +1, then there is a perfect positive correlation between the two variables. This lets us know that X is a perfect predictor of Y. When *r* is –1, then there is also a perfect correlation, but this time it is a perfect negative correlation. X is still a perfect predictor of Y, but in the opposite direction. For example, as age increases by 1 year, remaining life expectancy decreases by 1 year (controlling for external factors, ceteris paribus). When *r* is equal to zero, then there is absolutely no correlation between the two variables, as shown in Figure 11.1.

Bivariate Regression

Researchers are interested in predicting the value of the dependent variable (Y) from the information they have about the independent variable (X). This is called a bivariate regression analysis since it involves exactly two variables, one

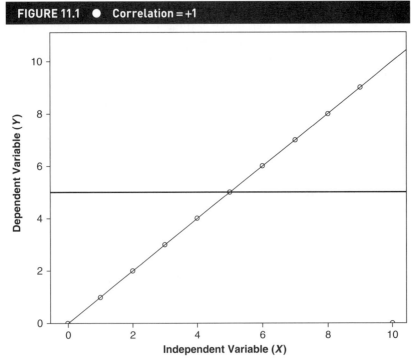

FIGURE 11.1 ● Correlation = +1

Note: The sloped line (slope = +1) represents the +1 correlation; the horizontal line represents a correlation of 0, where *Y* has the same value for any and all values of *X*.

independent variable and one dependent variable. The general format of the equation for bivariate regression is as follows:

$$\hat{Y} = bX + a$$

where

X represents the value of the independent variable
$\hat{Y}$ (called Y-hat, phonetically: why-hat) will return the predicted value for the dependent variable
b represents the slope of the regression line
a represents the y-intercept, the point at which the line crosses the y-axis

Statistical software can calculate regression equations very quickly. To do so by hand can take hours or days or become impossible with increasing numbers of data points and independent variables. SPSS, SAS, Stata, and even Excel are commonly used for this purpose. Our goal in this chapter is to help you understand the what and why of the statistic (discussed previously) and to be able to interpret it in a meaningful way (discussed next).

Suppose you are interested in studying the effect of education on personal income. We will use data from the General Social Survey (2014) to investigate that relationship. For our bivariate regression analysis, we can use the variable EDUC (years of education) as the independent variable and REALRINC as the dependent variable. Here are the results you will be given from your statistical software:

$$\hat{Y} = bX + a \rightarrow \hat{Y} = \$2{,}870.78X * - \$17{,}295.12 *$$

You will notice that each term has an asterisk (*). In written statistical results, this is an indication of statistical significance. In other words, there is a statistically significant relationship between X and Y. You can determine this by finding the appropriate p value in the statistical output you get from your statistical program. As an example, we will use the SPSS output shown in Table 11.1.

In the last column, "Sig.," the p value is given. Here, for both the constant, a, and the independent variable, b, the Sig. value is equal to zero (.000). If the cutoff for statistical significance is a p value of .05, then clearly this falls well below that and we can assign an asterisk in each such case. Of course, for different analyses you might set the p value for significance to another level. You will also notice that the a and b values, themselves, have been transferred from the Unstandardized Coefficients (B) column.

Looking back at the equation, we can begin further interpretation. Not only do we know that there is a statistically significant relationship between years of education (highest year of school completed) and respondent's annual income, but we can see the average impact that each additional year of education has on earnings. We can determine the direction and the magnitude of the predicted relationship.

---

*Statistically significant at the $p \le .05$ level.

TABLE 11.1 ● Bivariate Regression Coefficients from SPSS Statistics Output

		Unstandardized Coefficients		Standardized Coefficients		
Model		B	Std. Error	Beta	t	Sig.
1	(Constant)	−17295.116	3046.635		−5.677	.000
	HIGHEST YEAR OF SCHOOL COMPLETED	2870.784	210.896	.330	13.612	.000

Coefficients[a]

[a] Dependent Variable: RS INCOME IN CONSTANT $

General Interpretation: The *b* value provides this information. For a unit increase in X, there is a *b* increase in Y.

Specific Interpretation: For every 1 additional year of education, the average increase in annual income is $2,870.78.

The fine print: We have considerable prior knowledge about education, and so we know there are many other factors that can contribute to earnings beyond simply having spent an additional year in school, such as academic performance, college major, degree type, degrees completed, schools attended, and so on. Again, years of education does exhibit a statistically significant relationship with respondent's annual earnings, but is there a way we can assess the additive effects of additional variables or what percentage of the variation in earnings is explained by year of education? Yes! We can utilize a PRE statistic (as introduced in Chapter 9).

Coefficient of Determination (r^2)

Following up on the example from the section above, we can use another tool to assess the proportion of error that we have reduced (or, put another way, the amount of variation explained) in the relationship between the two variables under study, years of education and annual earnings. The coefficient of determination, r^2, is a PRE statistic for use with interval and ratio (continuous, scale) variables. The coefficient of determination (r^2) works in much the same way as gamma, Somers' *d*, and Kendall's tau-*b* that were discussed in Chapter 9. This should not come as any surprise, since r^2, like the others, is a PRE statistic and has the same underlying basis and purpose.

The coefficient of determination, r^2, is literally r^2, that is, Pearson's *r* times itself. Therefore, the range of r^2 is 0 to 1. If r^2 is equal to 1, then that means 100% of the variation in the dependent variable is explained by the variation in the independent variable (or, put another way, 100% of the error or uncertainty has been reduced/eliminated from our prediction of the dependent variable). If r^2 is equal to zero, then we also know that there is no correlation (zero times zero equals zero). In that case, absolutely none of the variation in the dependent variable is explained by the variation in the independent variable (or, from another perspective, with the use of the independent variable, we have not been able to eliminate any of the uncertainty/errors in predicting the dependent variable).

It is extremely rare that r^2 would actually ever be equal to the extremes of zero or 1. So, if r^2 is somewhere in between, how should it be interpreted? Returning to the example with years of education and annual income, you'll find sample output from SPSS in Table 11.2.

Not surprisingly, r^2 can be found in the column labeled "R Square." For this example, r^2 is equal to .109. This would be interpreted as follows: 10.9% of the variation in annual income is explained by years of education. Alternatively, we know that we have eliminated 10.9% of the errors in predicting annual income by utilizing knowledge of the respondents' number of years of education.

The total percent of "causes" for any given outcome must necessarily be equal to 100%. If you truly know everything that caused something, which is extremely rare, you would have a PRE value of 1.00 (whether it is r^2 or one of the other PRE statistics). However, we usually only have some of the information. Take the example presented in a pie chart in Figure 11.2. Why do students get certain grades in their statistics course? Do we know all 100% of the reasons? Unfortunately, no. However, we do know some of the noteworthy contributors. By utilizing those variables to calculate an r^2, we can account for a large share of the explanation. The data in Figure 11.2 are hypothetical, but realistic. Consider that even if the variations in attendance, study time, prior math classes, and going to the professor's office hours were to account for a hefty 80% of the variation in grades in statistics courses, there would still be 20% left to other explanations, or other independent variables. PRE explanations can always be considered in this pie chart format, where we have slices that tell us for how much explanation we can account, and the remaining "slice" represents the unknown or unmeasured factors. Sometimes, we may have ideas, but measurement or data collection may prevent us from obtaining

TABLE 11.2 ● Regression PRE Statistics (r^2) From SPSS Statistics Output

		Model Summary		
Model	r	r Square	Adjusted r Square	Std. Error of the Estimate
1	.330[a]	.109	.108	24,559.555

[a] Predictors: (Constant), HIGHEST YEAR OF SCHOOL COMPLETED.

FIGURE 11.2   ●   Contributing Factors to Student Academic Performance

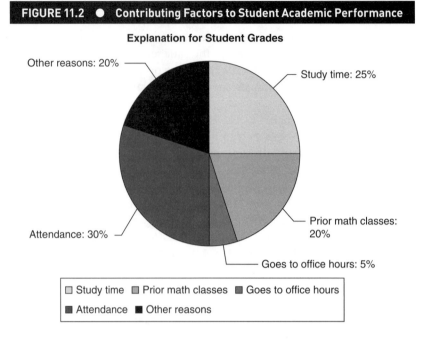

Explanation for Student Grades

Other reasons: 20%

Study time: 25%

Prior math classes: 20%

Attendance: 30%

Goes to office hours: 5%

☐ Study time ▨ Prior math classes ■ Goes to office hours
■ Attendance ■ Other reasons

that information. Also, the remaining explanation might be composed of a great many factors, and each may account for only a very small portion of variation in the dependent variable.

Having a value of .109 for r^2 is usually considered noteworthy. But what if you want to be able to eliminate a larger proportion of errors of prediction? For that, you will need more information about the respondents, in the form of additional variables. Having multiple independent variables may help improve the prediction. To find out, you will use multiple regression.

Multiple Regression

If you wish to include two or more independent variables (along with a dependent variable) in a regression analysis, you must use multiple regression. With statistical software, multiple regression is just as easy to do as bivariate regression. The only difference will be the addition of the name of the additional independent variable(s).

Variables That Can Be Analyzed in Regression Analysis

Remember that regression analyses require interval-ratio variables, so when incorporating variables such as sex/gender, race/ethnicity, religion, and others that are not at that level of measurement, it is important to use caution. This does not mean that we cannot include those variables, but it does mean that we need to treat them in particular ways, as described below.

For dichotomous variables, those that have exactly two attributes (categories), you can use those as independent variables because the cumulative property of levels of measurement (see Chapter 6) permits dichotomous variables to be treated like ratio variables.

Unfortunately, nominal-level variables with more than two attributes cannot be used in a regression analysis without careful preparation. This can be done by creating a set of dummy variables. A **dummy variable** is a variable with two attributes: 0 and 1; 0 indicates absence of a characteristic and 1 indicates its presence.

It is necessary to create a dummy variable for all but one of the attributes, the "omitted" comparison attribute, of the original nominal variable and use each of those dichotomies in the regression equation as independent variables. The number of dummy variables necessary for a given variable will be equal to $K - 1$, where K is the number of categories of the original variable. As explained earlier, dichotomies are an exception to the cumulative property of levels of measurement, which tells us that variables measured at higher levels can be treated at lower levels, but *not* vice versa. Dichotomies, typically considered categorical or nominal, can be treated as if they are at any level of measurement.

If we add the variable `sex` (gender) from the General Social Survey (2014) as a dummy variable, it would need to be coded 0 and 1, per the guidance above regarding dummy variables. In doing that, we have named it male (1 means the respondent is male; 0 means the respondent is not male). You could reverse the coding and name the variable female. From the SPSS output in Table 11.3, you can see that in this case, $r^2 = .172$, which means that 17.2% of the variation in respondent's real annual income (`realrinc`) is explained by the variation in the independent variables: years of education (`educ`) and gender (`male`). Note that the r^2 was just .109 earlier without the inclusion of gender.

The "Coefficients" table (in Table 11.4), again, provides the information that can be used to construct the regression model and equation. Note that the dummy variable, `male`, is also statistically significant at the $p \leq .05$ level.

TABLE 11.3 ● Regression PRE Statistics (r^2) From SPSS Statistics Output

Model Summary[a]			
Model	r	r Square	Adjusted r Square	Std. Error of the Estimate
1	.415[b]	.172	.171	23,677.751

[a] Dependent Variable: RS INCOME IN CONSTANT $.
[b] Predictors: (Constant), Male (or not), HIGHEST YEAR OF SCHOOL COMPLETED.

$$\hat{Y} = bX_1 + bX_2 + a \rightarrow \hat{Y} = \$2,993.54X_1 * + \$13,113.67X_2 * - \$25,488.11$$

The X_1 coefficient (educ, years of respondent's education) can be interpreted to mean that each additional year of education provides a \$2,993.54 predicted increase in real annual income. The X_2 coefficient (male, dummy variable for gender) can be interpreted to mean that males have a predicted real annual income of \$13,113.67 more than those who are not male. As you can see from the last column in the output table, both independent variables are statistically significant, with $p = .000$.

Interaction Effects

You can include an interaction effect in your regression model (equation). An interaction effect is some sort of pattern impacting the dependent variable when two or more independent variables are linked. A common way to do this is to take two variables thought to be responsible for an interaction effect and multiply them together as one of the independent variable terms in the equation. Since regression equations are additive, it does not register the impact of multiplication across variables unless you include an appropriate term in the equation for that purpose. Another way to think of this is that you are creating a new variable by multiplying two of the others together. Ultimately, you can construct a new variable from two variables by using other, nonadditive functions such as logarithms, exponentiation, and so on.

Mediating and Moderating Effects

A mediating variable is one that explains the relationship between a separate independent and dependent variable. A moderating variable is one that

TABLE 11.4 ● Multivariate Regression Coefficients from SPSS Statistics Output

Coefficients[a]					
	Unstandardized Coefficients		Standardized Coefficients		
Model	B	Std. Error	Beta	t	Sig.
(Constant)	−25488.106	3033.825		−8.401	.000
1 HIGHEST YEAR OF SCHOOL COMPLETED	2993.544	203.642	.344	14.700	.000
Male (or not)	13113.673	1215.483	.252	10.789	.000

[a] Dependent Variable: RS INCOME IN CONSTANT $.

*Statistically significant at the $p \leq .05$ level.

accounts for the strength (magnitude of the relationship) between a separate independent and dependent variable.

Logistic Regression

Like linear regression (OLS) analysis, logistic regression analysis allows us to predict values on a dependent variable from information that we have about other (independent) variables. **Logistic regression** analysis is also known as *logit* regression analysis, and it is performed on a dichotomous dependent variable and dichotomous independent variables. Through the use of dummy variables (introduced earlier and elaborated upon further below), it is possible to incorporate independent variables that have more than two categories. The dependent variable usually measures the presence of something or the likelihood that a future event will happen; examples include predictions of whether students will graduate on time or whether a student will graduate at all.

In this book, we cover binomial logistic regression. For variables that have more than two attributes (categories), you could explore the possibilities of multinomial logistic regression or ordinal logistic regression. They share many features of binomial logistic regression, including methods of interpretation.

Preparing Variables for Logistic Regression Analysis

In order to be able to compute a logistic regression model, the variables to be used should be dichotomous. Furthermore, they should be coded as "1," representing existence of an attribute, and "0" to denote nonexistence of that attribute. This may involve considerable recoding of the variables you intend to use. It will even require simpler transformations from dichotomies coded as "1" and "2" to dichotomies coded as "0" and "1."

For our logistic regression example, suppose we are interested in work status as predicted by gender and race/ethnicity. Earlier in this chapter, `male`, a dummy variable for sex, was created; the "1–2" dichotomy was transformed into a "0–1" dichotomy, where 0 = not male and 1 = male.

The General Social Survey variable `wrkstat` has eight categories, so we will need to decide what one category we want to examine. In recoding this variable, we create a variable that shows whether the respondent is (a) working full-time or (b) not working full-time.

Creating a Set of Dummy Variables

Our other independent variables will represent race/ethnicity. We will use the four-category race variable. The categories are White, Black, Other, and Hispanic. Because there are four categories, we will need to create and use *three* dummy variables. The number of dummy variables in a set that represents a nominal variable is equal to $K - 1$, where K is the number of categories of the original nominal/categorical variable.

Because the "Other" category is relatively small at just 6.6% of valid cases (and is a category comprised of respondents who, because of the nature of the "Other" category, are not necessarily similar with regard to race), you may wish to define those in that category as missing and proceed with a three-category variable (White, Black, and Hispanic), producing two dummy variables: $K - 1 = 2$.

As you create the dummy variables, remember that each one will have two categories (0 and 1). The number 1 will represent having that characteristic (dummy label), and 0 will represent an absence of that characteristic. So, the dummy variable "White" will be coded 1 for respondents who identify as White, and 0 for all others. "Black" will be coded 1 for respondents who identify as Black, and 0 for all others. "Hispanic" will be coded 1 for respondents who identify as Hispanic, and 0 for all others. So, for people who identify as Black, they would be coded 1 on the Black variable and 0 on *all* of the other dummy variables. It is important not to omit them or mark them as missing cases for the other dummy variables—make sure they are marked with a 0, indicating an absence of that attribute.

Interpreting Odds Ratios

Logistic regression uses natural logarithms to produce a logistic curve as a predictor, whereas you may remember that OLS linear regression uses the least squares method to produce a straight line as a predictor. The coefficients in a logistic regression model can be exponentiated as log odds ratios.

With logistic regression, r-squares (r^2) are presented: Cox and Snell as well as Nagelkerke. Although computed differently, these numbers can be interpreted in much the same way as r^2 itself, the coefficient of determination. These values are PRE statistics and can be interpreted as such.

With logistic regression, you will have both coefficients and exponentiated coefficients (SPSS labels this column as "Exp(B)." This value tells how much more or less likely a subject in the designated category is to be in the affirmative category on the dependent variable (employed full-time) than a subject in the omitted reference category.

For the coefficient male, the odds ratio is 1.811, and it is statistically significant ($p = 0.000$ in the "Sig." column); therefore, males are 1.811 times more likely than nonmales to be employed full-time and not fall into some other category of employment.

In this case, none of the race/ethnicity variables were statistically significant, but we can try to interpret an example as if they were. Suppose the dummy variable "Hispanic" has an exponentiated coefficient of 0.945. This would be interpreted as a comparison: Hispanics are only 0.945 times as likely as other groups to be employed full-time. If the exponentiated coefficient for Black is 1.139, that tells us that respondents who identified as Black are 1.139 times as likely to be employed full-time as others.

Step Models

To have SPSS Statistics (or other statistical software) help produce the equation with the best set of statistically significant variables, so that you will not need to try each combination manually, you can choose to request a step model. In SPSS, that is done by selecting a different option from the pull-down menu in the "Method" pane in the "Logistic Regression" dialog box, such as "Backward: Conditional," as demonstrated in the screenshot. The statistical software will go through one or more *steps* to ascertain the best logistic regression model to fit the data.

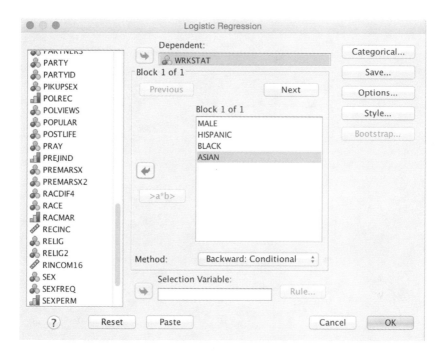

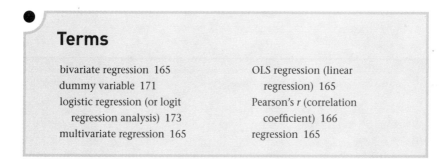

Terms

Indices, Typologies, and Scales

Indices, Typologies, and Scales Defined and Explained

Indices

A common method researchers use to operationalize constructs is by developing scales, indices, and typologies that help measure social concepts more accurately. The terms *index* and *scale* are often incorrectly used interchangeably, primarily because they are both summative measurements of a construct. However, they are different in their approach to measurement.

An **index** is a measurement that is built on individual, real-world indicators of a social construct. For example, if researchers wanted to study how sexual communication (independent variable) is associated with marital satisfaction (dependent variable), they might want to know in which types of sexual activities couples have engaged over a period of time to better understand the relationship between sexual communication and marital satisfaction. In this case, it would be problematic to ask an individual, "How is your sexual communication with your partner?" Instead, an index of "sexual communication" might include measures such as those in Box 12.1. Taking a count of specific behaviors would lead to a number of sexual communication behaviors one has used. This index helps quantify and identify sexual communication.

BOX 12.1
SEXUAL COMMUNICATION INDEX

One example of an index uses individuals' sexual communication based on their responses to the following question: *"In the past month*, have you and your partner talked about sex in any of the following ways?"* (1) *I asked for something in bed*; (2) *My partner asked for something in bed*; (3) *One of us praised the other*; (4) *One of us asked for feedback*; (5) *One of us called, e-mailed, or texted to tease*; (6) *One of us gently criticized the other in bed*. When each of the selected items is coded as 1, an index can be created. In this case, the index would indicate the number of communication strategies used in the past month, ranging from 1 to 6.

Typologies

A **typology** is a composite measure that uses discrete categories based on information from one or more variables. Building on the previous example, a sex researcher might want to identify types of married couples based on their sex frequency and sexual satisfaction (Gillespie, 2016a, 2016b). As such, the researcher might use information from two different variables—sex frequency and sexual satisfaction—to create a typology: (1) those who report having frequent and satisfying sex, (2) those who report having frequent but unsatisfying sex, (3) those who report having infrequent but satisfying sex, and (4) those who report having infrequent and unsatisfying sex. This is understood to be a typology because it situates individuals into four specific "types," or categorical groups.

Scales

A **scale** is another composite measure that is based on multiple measures of a latent construct. For example, religiosity is a term used in the social sciences to indicate an individual's level of religiousness. This multidimensional construct can form a scale. For example, rather than asking an individual about how religious he or she is, one might instead measure how religious an individual is across a number of dimensions (e.g., spirituality, religious behavior, and attitudes toward religion) in order to form a scale of religiosity (an unobservable, overall level of religiousness). Table 12.1 presents a scale for the multidimensional measurement of religiosity.

TABLE 12.1 ● Religiosity Scale	Strongly Agree	Agree	Neutral	Disagree	Strongly Disagree
Religion is important in my life. (Attitudinal Dimension)	1	2	3	4	5
I regularly attend religious services. (Behavioral Dimension)	1	2	3	4	5
I feel connected to a higher power. (Spiritual Dimension)	1	2	3	4	5
Religion is the one true path to eternal life. (Attitudinal)	1	2	3	4	5
I frequently read religious literature. (Behavioral)	1	2	3	4	5
I believe that religion is sacred. (Spiritual)	1	2	3	4	5

In this case, a researcher can average across several indicators to target the concept of religiosity. Consistency between the items can be assessed using Cronbach's alpha, which was discussed in Chapter 8.

Whether measurements are based on a scale, an index, or a typology, researchers always want to confirm that their research design is sound and they are measuring what they intend to measure in a strategic and consistent way.

Terms

index 177
scale 178

typology 178

References

Gillespie, B. J. (2016a). Correlates of sex frequency and sexual satisfaction among partnered older adults. *Journal of Sex & Marital Therapy, 43*(5), 402–423.

Gillespie, B. J. (2016b). Sexual synchronicity and communication among partnered older adults. *Journal of Sex & Marital Therapy, 43*(5), 441–455.

• Appendix A •

The Standard Normal Table

The values in column A are z scores. Column B lists the proportion of area between the mean and a given z. Column C lists the proportion of area beyond a given z. Only positive z scores are listed. Because the normal curve is symmetrical, the areas for negative z scores will be exactly the same as the areas for positive z scores.

TABLE A.1 ● The Standard Normal Table

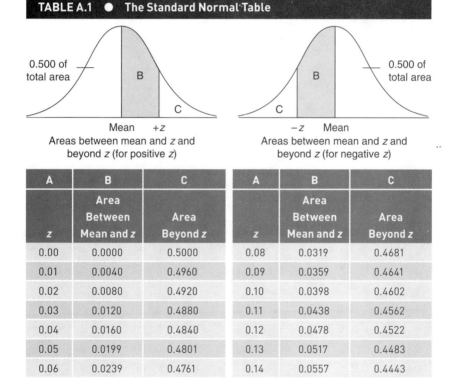

Areas between mean and z and beyond z (for positive z)

Areas between mean and z and beyond z (for negative z)

A	B	C	A	B	C
z	Area Between Mean and z	Area Beyond z	z	Area Between Mean and z	Area Beyond z
0.00	0.0000	0.5000	0.08	0.0319	0.4681
0.01	0.0040	0.4960	0.09	0.0359	0.4641
0.02	0.0080	0.4920	0.10	0.0398	0.4602
0.03	0.0120	0.4880	0.11	0.0438	0.4562
0.04	0.0160	0.4840	0.12	0.0478	0.4522
0.05	0.0199	0.4801	0.13	0.0517	0.4483
0.06	0.0239	0.4761	0.14	0.0557	0.4443
0.07	0.0279	0.4721	0.15	0.0596	0.4404

(Continued)

TABLE A.1 ● (Continued)

A	B	C	A	B	C
z	Area Between Mean and z	Area Beyond z	z	Area Between Mean and z	Area Beyond z
0.16	0.0636	0.4364	0.49	0.1879	0.3121
0.17	0.0675	0.4325	0.50	0.1915	0.3085
0.18	0.0714	0.4286	0.51	0.1950	0.3050
0.19	0.0753	0.4247	0.52	0.1985	0.3015
0.20	0.0793	0.4207	0.53	0.2019	0.2981
0.21	0.0832	0.4168	0.54	0.2054	0.2946
0.22	0.0871	0.4129	0.55	0.2088	0.2912
0.23	0.0910	0.4090	0.56	0.2123	0.2877
0.24	0.0948	0.4052	0.57	0.2157	0.2843
0.25	0.0987	0.4013	0.58	0.2190	0.2810
0.26	0.1026	0.3974	0.59	0.2224	0.2776
0.27	0.1064	0.3936	0.60	0.2257	0.2743
0.28	0.1103	0.3897	0.61	0.2291	0.2709
0.29	0.1141	0.3859	0.62	0.2324	0.2676
0.30	0.1179	0.3821	0.63	0.2357	0.2643
0.31	0.1217	0.3783	0.64	0.2389	0.2611
0.32	0.1255	0.3745	0.65	0.2422	0.2578
0.33	0.1293	0.3707	0.66	0.2454	0.2546
0.34	0.1331	0.3669	0.67	0.2486	0.2514
0.35	0.1368	0.3632	0.68	0.2517	0.2483
0.36	0.1406	0.3594	0.69	0.2549	0.2451
0.37	0.1443	0.3557	0.70	0.2580	0.2420
0.38	0.1480	0.3520	0.71	0.2611	0.2389
0.39	0.1517	0.3483	0.72	0.2642	0.2358
0.40	0.1554	0.3446	0.73	0.2673	0.2327
0.41	0.1591	0.3409	0.74	0.2703	0.2297
0.42	0.1628	0.3372	0.75	0.2734	0.2266
0.43	0.1664	0.3336	0.76	0.2764	0.2236
0.44	0.1700	0.3300	0.77	0.2794	0.2206
0.45	0.1736	0.3264	0.78	0.2823	0.2177
0.46	0.1772	0.3228	0.79	0.2852	0.2148
0.47	0.1808	0.3192	0.80	0.2881	0.2119
0.48	0.1844	0.3156	0.81	0.2910	0.2090

A	B	C	A	B	C
z	Area Between Mean and z	Area Beyond z	z	Area Between Mean and z	Area Beyond z
0.82	0.2939	0.2061	1.15	0.3749	0.1251
0.83	0.2967	0.2033	1.16	0.3770	0.1230
0.84	0.2995	0.2005	1.17	0.3790	0.1210
0.85	0.3023	0.1977	1.18	0.3810	0.1190
0.86	0.3051	0.1949	1.19	0.3830	0.1170
0.87	0.3078	0.1992	1.20	0.3849	0.1151
0.88	0.3106	0.1894	1.21	0.3869	0.1131
0.89	0.3133	0.1867	1.22	0.3888	0.1112
0.90	0.3159	0.1841	1.23	0.3907	0.1093
0.91	0.3186	0.1814	1.24	0.3925	0.1075
0.92	0.3212	0.1788	1.25	0.3944	0.1056
0.93	0.3238	0.1762	1.26	0.3962	0.1038
0.94	0.3264	0.1736	1.27	0.3980	0.1020
0.95	0.3289	0.1711	1.28	0.3997	0.1003
0.96	0.3315	0.1685	1.29	0.4015	0.0985
0.97	0.3340	0.1660	1.30	0.4032	0.0968
0.98	0.3365	0.1635	1.31	0.4049	0.0951
0.99	0.3389	0.1611	1.32	0.4066	0.0934
1.00	0.3413	0.1587	1.33	0.4082	0.0918
1.01	0.3438	0.1562	1.34	0.4099	0.0901
1.02	0.3461	0.1539	1.35	0.4115	0.0885
1.03	0.3485	0.1515	1.36	0.4131	0.0869
1.04	0.3508	0.1492	1.37	0.4147	0.0853
1.05	0.3531	0.1469	1.38	0.4612	0.0838
1.06	0.3554	0.1446	1.39	0.4177	0.0823
1.07	0.3577	0.1423	1.40	0.4192	0.0808
1.08	0.3599	0.1401	1.41	0.4207	0.0793
1.09	0.3621	0.1379	1.42	0.4222	0.0778
1.10	0.3643	0.1357	1.43	0.4236	0.0764
1.11	0.3665	0.1335	1.44	0.4251	0.0749
1.12	0.3686	0.1314	1.45	0.4265	0.0735
1.13	0.3708	0.1292	1.46	0.4279	0.0721
1.14	0.3729	0.1271	1.47	0.4292	0.0708

(Continued)

TABLE A.1 ● (Continued)

A	B	C	A	B	C
z	Area Between Mean and z	Area Beyond z	z	Area Between Mean and z	Area Beyond z
1.48	0.4306	0.0694	1.81	0.4649	0.0351
1.49	0.4319	0.0681	1.82	0.4656	0.0344
1.50	0.4332	0.0668	1.83	0.4664	0.0336
1.51	0.4345	0.0655	1.84	0.4671	0.0329
1.52	0.4357	0.0643	1.85	0.4678	0.0322
1.53	0.4370	0.0630	1.86	0.4686	0.0314
1.54	0.4382	0.0618	1.87	0.4693	0.0307
1.55	0.4394	0.0606	1.88	0.4699	0.0301
1.56	0.4406	0.0594	1.89	0.4706	0.0294
1.57	0.4418	0.0582	1.90	0.4713	0.0287
1.58	0.4429	0.0571	1.91	0.4719	0.0281
1.59	0.4441	0.0559	1.92	0.4726	0.0274
1.60	0.4452	0.0548	1.93	0.4732	0.0268
1.61	0.4463	0.0537	1.94	0.4738	0.0262
1.62	0.4474	0.0526	1.95	0.4744	0.0256
1.63	0.4484	0.0516	1.96	0.4750	0.0250
1.64	0.4495	0.0505	1.97	0.4756	0.0244
1.65	0.4505	0.0495	1.98	0.4761	0.0239
1.66	0.4515	0.0485	1.99	0.4767	0.0233
1.67	0.4525	0.0475	2.00	0.4772	0.0228
1.68	0.4535	0.0465	2.01	0.4778	0.0222
1.69	0.4545	0.0455	2.02	0.4783	0.0217
1.70	0.4554	0.0466	2.03	0.4788	0.0212
1.71	0.4564	0.0436	2.04	0.4793	0.0207
1.72	0.4573	0.0427	2.05	0.4798	0.0202
1.73	0.4582	0.0418	2.06	0.4803	0.0197
1.74	0.4591	0.0409	2.07	0.4808	0.0192
1.75	0.4599	0.0401	2.08	0.4812	0.0188
1.76	0.4608	0.0392	2.09	0.4817	0.0183
1.77	0.4616	0.0384	2.10	0.4821	0.0179
1.78	0.4625	0.0375	2.11	0.4826	0.0174
1.79	0.4633	0.0367	2.12	0.4830	0.0170
1.80	0.4641	0.0359	2.13	0.4834	0.0166

A z	B Area Between Mean and z	C Area Beyond z	A z	B Area Between Mean and z	C Area Beyond z
2.14	0.4838	0.0162	2.47	0.4932	0.0068
2.15	0.4842	0.0158	2.48	0.4934	0.0066
2.16	0.4846	0.0154	2.49	0.4936	0.0064
2.17	0.4850	0.0150	2.50	0.4938	0.0062
2.18	0.4854	0.0146	2.51	0.4940	0.0060
2.19	0.4857	0.0143	2.52	0.4941	0.0059
2.20	0.4861	0.0139	2.53	0.4943	0.0057
2.21	0.4864	0.0136	2.54	0.4945	0.0055
2.22	0.4868	0.0132	2.55	0.4946	0.0054
2.23	0.4871	0.0129	2.56	0.4948	0.0052
2.24	0.4875	0.0125	2.57	0.4949	0.0051
2.25	0.4878	0.0122	2.58	0.4951	0.0049
2.26	0.4881	0.0119	2.59	0.4952	0.0048
2.27	0.4884	0.0116	2.60	0.4953	0.0047
2.28	0.4887	0.0113	2.61	0.4955	0.0045
2.29	0.4890	0.0110	2.62	0.4956	0.0044
2.30	0.4893	0.0107	2.63	0.4957	0.0043
2.31	0.4896	0.0104	2.64	0.4959	0.0041
2.32	0.4898	0.0102	2.65	0.4960	0.0040
2.33	0.4901	0.0099	2.66	0.4961	0.0039
2.34	0.4904	0.0096	2.67	0.4962	0.0038
2.35	0.4906	0.0094	2.68	0.4963	0.0037
2.36	0.4909	0.0091	2.69	0.4964	0.0036
2.37	0.4911	0.0089	2.70	0.4965	0.0035
2.38	0.4913	0.0087	2.71	0.4966	0.0034
2.39	0.4916	0.0084	2.72	0.4967	0.0033
2.40	0.4918	0.0082	2.73	0.4968	0.0032
2.41	0.4920	0.0080	2.74	0.4969	0.0031
2.42	0.4922	0.0078	2.75	0.4970	0.0030
2.43	0.4925	0.0075	2.76	0.4971	0.0029
2.44	0.4927	0.0073	2.77	0.4972	0.0028
2.45	0.4929	0.0071	2.78	0.4973	0.0027
2.46	0.4931	0.0069	2.79	0.4974	0.0026

(Continued)

TABLE A.1 ● (Continued)

z	Area Between Mean and z	Area Beyond z	z	Area Between Mean and z	Area Beyond z
2.80	0.4974	0.0026	3.11	0.4991	0.0009
2.81	0.4975	0.0025	3.12	0.4991	0.0009
2.82	0.4976	0.0024	3.13	0.4991	0.0009
2.83	0.4977	0.0023	3.14	0.4992	0.0008
2.84	0.4977	0.0023	3.15	0.4992	0.0008
2.85	0.4978	0.0022	3.16	0.4992	0.0008
2.86	0.4979	0.0021	3.17	0.4992	0.0008
2.87	0.4979	0.0021	3.18	0.4993	0.0007
2.88	0.4980	0.0020	3.19	0.4993	0.0007
2.89	0.4981	0.0019	3.20	0.4993	0.0007
2.90	0.4981	0.0019	3.21	0.4993	0.0007
2.91	0.4982	0.0018	3.22	0.4994	0.0006
2.92	0.4982	0.0018	3.23	0.4994	0.0006
2.93	0.4983	0.0017	3.24	0.4994	0.0006
2.94	0.4984	0.0016	3.25	0.4994	0.0006
2.95	0.4984	0.0016	3.26	0.4994	0.0006
2.96	0.4985	0.0015	3.27	0.4995	0.0005
2.97	0.4985	0.0015	3.28	0.4995	0.0005
2.98	0.4986	0.0014	3.29	0.4995	0.0005
2.99	0.4986	0.0014	3.30	0.4995	0.0005
3.00	0.4986	0.0014	3.31	0.4995	0.0005
3.01	0.4987	0.0013	3.32	0.4995	0.0005
3.02	0.4987	0.0013	3.33	0.4996	0.0004
3.03	0.4988	0.0012	3.34	0.4996	0.0004
3.04	0.4988	0.0012	3.35	0.4996	0.0004
3.05	0.4989	0.0011	3.36	0.4996	0.0004
3.06	0.4989	0.0011	3.37	0.4996	0.0004
3.07	0.4989	0.0011	3.38	0.4996	0.0004
3.08	0.4990	0.0010	3.39	0.4997	0.0003
3.09	0.4990	0.0010	3.40	0.4997	0.0003
3.10	0.4990	0.0010	3.41	0.4997	0.0003

A	B	C	A	B	C
z	Area Between Mean and z	Area Beyond z	z	Area Between Mean and z	Area Beyond z
3.42	0.4997	0.0003	3.49	0.4998	0.0002
3.43	0.4997	0.0003	3.50	0.4998	0.0002
3.44	0.4997	0.0003	3.60	0.4998	0.0002
3.45	0.4997	0.0003	3.70	0.4999	0.0001
3.46	0.4997	0.0003	3.80	0.4999	0.0001
3.47	0.4997	0.0003	3.90	0.4999	<0.0001
3.48	0.4997	0.0003	4.00	0.4999	<0.0001

Source: Frankfort-Nachmias, C., & Leon-Guerrero, A. (2017). *Social statistics for a diverse society* (8th ed.). Thousand Oaks, CA: Sage.

• Appendix B •

Critical Values for *t* Statistic

How to use this table:

1. Compute the *t* value test statistic.

2. Compare the obtained *t* value with the critical value listed in this table. Be sure you have calculated the number of degrees of freedom correctly and you have selected an appropriate level of significance.

3. If the obtained value is greater than the critical or tabled value, the null hypothesis (that the means are equal) is not the most attractive explanation for any observed differences.

4. If the obtained value is less than the critical or table value, the null hypothesis is the most attractive explanation for any observed differences.

TABLE B.1 ● *t* Values Needed for Rejection of the Null Hypothesis

	One-Tailed Test				Two-Tailed Test		
df	0.10	0.05	0.01	df	0.10	0.05	0.01
1	3.078	6.314	31.821	1	6.314	12.706	63.657
2	1.886	2.92	6.965	2	2.92	4.303	9.925
3	1.638	2.353	4.541	3	2.353	3.182	5.841
4	1.533	2.132	3.747	4	2.132	2.776	4.604
5	1.476	2.015	3.365	5	2.015	2.571	4.032
6	1.44	1.943	3.143	6	1.943	2.447	3.708
7	1.415	1.895	2.998	7	1.895	2.365	3.5
8	1.397	1.86	2.897	8	1.86	2.306	3.356
9	1.383	1.833	2.822	9	1.833	2.262	3.25
10	1.372	1.813	2.764	10	1.813	2.228	3.17
11	1.364	1.796	2.718	11	1.796	2.201	3.106
12	1.356	1.783	2.681	12	1.783	2.179	3.055

(Continued)

TABLE B.1 ● (Continued)

df	One-Tailed Test 0.10	0.05	0.01	df	Two-Tailed Test 0.10	0.05	0.01
13	1.35	1.771	2.651	13	1.771	2.161	3.013
14	1.345	1.762	2.625	14	1.762	2.145	2.977
15	1.341	1.753	2.603	15	1.753	2.132	2.947
16	1.337	1.746	2.584	16	1.746	2.12	2.921
17	1.334	1.74	2.567	17	1.74	2.11	2.898
18	1.331	1.734	2.553	18	1.734	2.101	2.879
19	1.328	1.729	2.54	19	1.729	2.093	2.861
20	1.326	1.725	2.528	20	1.725	2.086	2.846
21	1.323	1.721	2.518	21	1.721	2.08	2.832
22	1.321	1.717	2.509	22	1.717	2.074	2.819
23	1.32	1.714	2.5	23	1.714	2.069	2.808
24	1.318	1.711	2.492	24	1.711	2.064	2.797
25	1.317	1.708	2.485	25	1.708	2.06	2.788
26	1.315	1.706	2.479	26	1.706	2.056	2.779
27	1.314	1.704	2.473	27	1.704	2.052	2.771
28	1.313	1.701	2.467	28	1.701	2.049	2.764
29	1.312	1.699	2.462	29	1.699	2.045	2.757
30	1.311	1.698	2.458	30	1.698	2.043	2.75
35	1.306	1.69	2.438	35	1.69	2.03	2.724
40	1.303	1.684	2.424	40	1.684	2.021	2.705
45	1.301	1.68	2.412	45	1.68	2.014	2.69
50	1.299	1.676	2.404	50	1.676	2.009	2.678
55	1.297	1.673	2.396	55	1.673	2.004	2.668
60	1.296	1.671	2.39	60	1.671	2.001	2.661
65	1.295	1.669	2.385	65	1.669	1.997	2.654
70	1.294	1.667	2.381	70	1.667	1.995	2.648
75	1.293	1.666	2.377	75	1.666	1.992	2.643
80	1.292	1.664	2.374	80	1.664	1.99	2.639
85	1.292	1.663	2.371	85	1.663	1.989	2.635
90	1.291	1.662	2.369	90	1.662	1.987	2.632
95	1.291	1.661	2.366	95	1.661	1.986	2.629
100	1.29	1.66	2.364	100	1.66	1.984	2.626
Infinity	1.282	1.645	2.327	Infinity	1.645	1.96	2.576

Source: Salkind, N. J. (2017). *Statistics for people who (think they) hate statistics* (6th ed.). Thousand Oaks, CA: Sage.

• Appendix C •

Critical Values for Chi-Square

How to use this table:

1. Compute the χ^2 value.

2. Determine the number of degrees of freedom for the *rows* $(r - 1)$ and the number of degrees of freedom for the *columns* $(c - 1)$. If your table is one-dimensional, then you have only columns.

3. Locate the critical value by locating the degrees of freedom in the *df* column. Then read across to the appropriate column for level of significance.

4. If the obtained value is greater than the critical or tabled value, the null hypothesis (that the frequencies are equal to one another) is not the most attractive explanation for any observed differences.

5. If the obtained value is less than the critical or tabled value, the null hypothesis is the most attractive explanation for any observed differences.

TABLE C.1 ● Critical Values for the Chi-Square Test			
Level of Significance			
df	.10	.05	.01
1	2.71	3.84	6.64
2	4.00	5.99	9.21
3	6.25	7.82	11.34
4	7.78	9.49	13.28
5	9.24	11.07	15.09
6	10.64	12.59	16.81
7	12.02	14.07	18.48
8	13.36	15.51	20.09

(Continued)

TABLE C.1 ● (Continued)			
Level of Significance			
df	.10	.05	.01
9	14.68	16.92	21.67
10	16.99	18.31	23.21
11	17.28	19.68	24.72
12	18.65	21.03	26.22
13	19.81	22.36	27.69
14	21.06	23.68	29.14
15	22.31	25.00	30.58
16	23.54	26.30	32.00
17	24.77	27.60	33.41
18	25.99	28.87	34.80
19	27.20	30.14	36.19
20	28.41	31.41	37.57
21	29.62	32.67	38.93
22	30.81	33.92	40.29
23	32.01	35.17	41.64
24	33.20	36.42	42.98
25	34.38	37.65	44.81
26	35.56	38.88	45.64
27	36.74	40.11	46.96
28	37.92	41.34	48.28
29	39.09	42.56	49.59
30	40.26	43.77	50.89

Source: Salkind, N. J. (2017). *Statistics for people who (think they) hate statistics* (6th ed.). Thousand Oaks, CA: Sage.

• Appendix D •

Critical Values for *F* Statistics

How to use this table:

1. Compute the *F* value.

2. Determine the number of degrees of freedom for the numerator $(k - 1)$ and the number of degrees of freedom for the denominator $(n - k)$.

3. Locate the critical value by reading across to locate the degrees of freedom in the numerator and down to locate the degrees of freedom in the denominator. The critical value is at the intersection of this column and row.

4. If the obtained value is greater than the critical or tabled value, the null hypothesis (that the means are equal to one another) is not the most attractive explanation for any observed differences.

5. If the obtained value is less than the critical or tabled value, the null hypothesis is the most attractive explanation for any observed differences.

TABLE D.1 ● Critical Values for Analysis of Variance or *F* Test

df for the Denominator	Type I Error Rate	*df* for the Numerator					
		1	2	3	4	5	6
1	.01	4052.00	4999.00	5403.00	5625.00	5764.00	5859.00
	.05	162.00	200.00	216.00	225.00	230.00	234.00
	.10	39.90	49.50	53.60	55.80	57.20	58.20
2	.01	98.50	99.00	99.17	99.25	99.30	99.33
	.05	18.51	19.00	19.17	19.25	19.30	19.33
	.10	8.53	9.00	9.16	9.24	9.29	9.33

(Continued)

193

TABLE D.1 ● (Continued)

df for the Denominator	Type I Error Rate	df for the Numerator					
		1	2	3	4	5	6
3	.01	34.12	30.82	29.46	28.71	28.24	27.91
	.05	10.13	9.55	9.28	9.12	9.01	8.94
	.10	5.54	5.46	5.39	5.34	5.31	5.28
4	.01	21.20	18.00	16.70	15.98	15.52	15.21
	.05	7.71	6.95	6.59	6.39	6.26	6.16
	.10	0.55	4.33	4.19	4.11	4.05	4.01
5	.01	16.26	13.27	12.06	11.39	10.97	10.67
	.05	6.61	5.79	5.41	5.19	5.05	4.95
	.10	4.06	3.78	3.62	3.52	3.45	3.41
6	.01	13.75	10.93	9.78	9.15	8.75	8.47
	.05	5.99	5.14	4.76	4.53	4.39	4.28
	.10	3.78	3.46	3.29	3.18	3.11	3.06
7	.01	12.25	9.55	8.45	7.85	7.46	7.19
	.05	5.59	4.74	4.35	4.12	3.97	3.87
	.10	3.59	3.26	3.08	2.96	2.88	2.83
8	.01	11.26	8.65	7.59	7.01	6.63	6.37
	.05	5.32	4.46	4.07	3.84	3.69	3.58
	.10	3.46	3.11	2.92	2.81	2.73	2.67
9	.01	10.56	8.02	6.99	6.42	6.06	5.80
	.05	5.12	4.26	3.86	3.63	3.48	3.37
	.10	3.36	3.01	2.81	2.69	2.61	2.55
10	.01	10.05	7.56	6.55	6.00	5.64	5.39
	.05	4.97	4.10	3.71	3.48	3.33	3.22
	.10	3.29	2.93	2.73	2.61	2.52	2.46
11	.01	9.65	7.21	6.22	5.67	5.32	5.07
	.05	4.85	3.98	3.59	3.36	3.20	3.10
	.10	3.23	2.86	2.66	2.54	2.45	2.39
12	.01	9.33	6.93	5.95	5.41	5.07	4.82
	.05	4.75	3.89	3.49	3.26	3.11	3.00
	.10	3.18	2.81	2.61	2.48	2.40	2.33
13	.01	9.07	6.70	5.74	5.21	4.86	4.62
	.05	4.67	3.81	3.41	3.18	3.03	2.92
	.10	3.14	2.76	2.56	2.43	2.35	2.28

df for the Denominator	Type I Error Rate	*df* for the Numerator					
		1	2	3	4	5	6
14	.01	8.86	6.52	5.56	5.04	4.70	4.46
	.05	4.60	3.74	3.34	3.11	2.96	2.85
	.10	3.10	2.73	2.52	2.40	2.31	2.24
15	.01	8.68	6.36	5.42	4.89	4.56	4.32
	.05	4.54	3.68	3.29	3.06	2.90	2.79
	.10	3.07	2.70	2.49	2.36	2.27	2.21
16	.01	8.53	6.23	5.29	4.77	4.44	4.20
	.05	4.49	3.63	3.24	3.01	2.85	2.74
	.10	3.05	2.67	2.46	2.33	2.24	2.18
17	.01	8.40	6.11	5.19	4.67	4.34	4.10
	.05	4.45	3.59	3.20	2.97	2.81	2.70
	.10	3.03	2.65	2.44	2.31	2.22	2.15
18	.01	8.29	6.01	5.09	4.58	4.25	4.02
	.05	4.41	3.56	3.16	2.93	2.77	2.66
	.10	3.01	2.62	2.42	2.29	2.20	2.13
19	.01	8.19	5.93	5.01	4.50	4.17	3.94
	.05	4.38	3.52	3.13	2.90	2.74	2.63
	.10	2.99	2.61	2.40	2.27	2.18	2.11
20	.01	8.10	5.85	4.94	4.43	4.10	3.87
	.05	4.35	3.49	3.10	2.87	2.71	2.60
	.10	2.98	2.59	2.38	2.25	2.16	2.09
21	.01	8.02	5.78	4.88	4.37	4.04	3.81
	.05	4.33	3.47	3.07	2.84	2.69	2.57
	.10	2.96	2.58	2.37	2.23	2.14	2.08
22	.01	7.95	5.72	4.82	4.31	3.99	3.76
	.05	4.30	3.44	3.05	2.82	2.66	2.55
	.10	2.95	2.56	2.35	2.22	2.13	2.06
23	.01	7.88	5.66	4.77	4.26	3.94	3.71
	.05	4.28	3.42	3.03	2.80	2.64	2.53
	.10	2.94	2.55	2.34	2.21	2.12	2.05
24	.01	7.82	5.61	4.72	4.22	3.90	3.67
	.05	4.26	3.40	3.01	2.78	2.62	2.51
	.10	2.93	2.54	2.33	2.20	2.10	2.04

(Continued)

TABLE D.1 ● (Continued)

df for the Denominator	Type I Error Rate	df for the Numerator					
		1	2	3	4	5	6
25	.01	7.77	5.57	4.68	4.18	3.86	3.63
	.05	4.24	3.39	2.99	2.76	2.60	2.49
	.10	2.92	2.53	2.32	2.19	2.09	2.03
26	.01	7.72	5.53	4.64	4.14	3.82	3.59
	.05	4.23	3.37	2.98	2.74	2.59	2.48
	.10	2.91	2.52	2.31	2.18	2.08	2.01
27	.01	7.68	5.49	4.60	4.11	3.79	3.56
	.05	4.21	3.36	2.96	2.73	2.57	2.46
	.10	2.90	2.51	2.30	2.17	2.07	2.01
28	.01	7.64	5.45	4.57	4.08	3.75	3.53
	.05	4.20	3.34	2.95	2.72	2.56	2.45
	.10	2.89	2.50	2.29	2.16	2.07	2.00
29	.01	7.60	5.42	4.54	4.05	3.73	3.50
	.05	4.18	3.33	2.94	2.70	2.55	2.43
	.10	2.89	2.50	2.28	2.15	2.06	1.99
30	.01	7.56	5.39	4.51	4.02	3.70	3.47
	.05	4.17	3.32	2.92	2.69	2.53	2.42
	.10	2.88	2.49	2.28	2.14	2.05	1.98
35	.01	7.42	5.27	4.40	3.91	3.59	3.37
	.05	4.12	3.27	2.88	2.64	2.49	2.37
	.10	2.86	2.46	2.25	2.14	2.02	1.95
40	.01	7.32	5.18	4.31	3.91	3.51	3.29
	.05	4.09	3.23	2.84	2.64	2.45	2.34
	.10	2.84	2.44	2.23	2.11	2.00	1.93
45	.01	7.23	5.11	4.25	3.83	3.46	3.23
	.05	4.06	3.21	2.81	2.61	2.42	2.31
	.10	2.82	2.43	2.21	2.09	1.98	1.91
50	.01	7.17	5.06	4.20	3.77	3.41	3.19
	.05	4.04	3.18	2.79	2.58	2.40	2.29
	.10	2.81	2.41	2.20	2.08	1.97	1.90
55	.01	7.12	5.01	4.16	3.72	3.37	3.15
	.05	4.02	3.17	2.77	2.56	2.38	2.27
	.10	2.80	2.40	2.19	2.06	1.96	1.89

df for the Denominator	Type I Error Rate	*df* for the Numerator					
		1	2	3	4	5	6
60	.01	7.08	4.98	4.13	3.68	3.34	3.12
	.05	4.00	3.15	2.76	2.54	2.37	2.26
	.10	2.79	2.39	2.18	2.05	1.95	1.88
65	.01	7.04	4.95	4.10	3.65	3.31	3.09
	.05	3.99	3.14	2.75	2.53	2.36	2.24
	.10	2.79	2.39	2.17	2.04	1.94	1.87
70	.01	7.01	4.92	4.08	3.62	3.29	3.07
	.05	3.98	3.13	2.74	2.51	2.35	2.23
	.10	2.78	2.38	2.16	2.03	1.93	1.86
75	.01	6.99	4.90	4.06	3.60	3.27	3.05
	.05	3.97	3.12	2.73	2.50	2.34	2.22
	.10	2.77	2.38	2.16	2.03	1.93	1.86
80	.01	3.96	4.88	4.04	3.56	3.26	3.04
	.05	6.96	3.11	2.72	2.49	2.33	2.22
	.10	2.77	2.37	2.15	2.02	1.92	1.85
85	.01	6.94	4.86	4.02	3.55	3.24	3.02
	.05	3.95	3.10	2.71	2.48	2.32	2.21
	.10	2.77	2.37	2.15	2.01	1.92	1.85
90	.01	6.93	4.85	4.02	3.54	3.23	3.01
	.05	3.95	3.10	2.71	2.47	2.32	2.20
	.10	2.76	2.36	2.15	2.01	1.91	1.84
95	.01	6.91	4.84	4.00	3.52	3.22	3.00
	.05	3.94	3.09	2.70	2.47	2.31	2.20
	.10	2.76	2.36	2.14	2.01	1.91	1.84
100	.01	6.90	4.82	3.98	3.51	3.21	2.99
	.05	3.94	3.09	2.70	2.46	2.31	2.19
	.10	2.76	2.36	2.14	2.00	1.91	1.83
Infinity	.01	6.64	4.61	3.78	3.32	3.02	2.80
	.05	3.84	3.00	2.61	2.37	2.22	2.10
	.10	2.71	2.30	2.08	1.95	1.85	1.78

Source: Salkind, N. J. (2017). *Statistics for people who (think they) hate statistics* (6th ed.). Thousand Oaks, CA: Sage.

• Appendix E •
Glossary

absolute frequencies: the number of cases in a particular category or range.

alpha: the cutoff probability a researcher allows for erroneously rejecting the null hypothesis when the null hypothesis is true.

alternate forms reliability: refers to consistency between two different versions of a measure that probes the same construct

alternative hypothesis (H_a): the opposite of the null hypothesis; this is a statement that there *is* a relationship between the independent variable(s) and the dependent variable.

analysis of variance (ANOVA): tests for differences in mean scores across independent groups.

a priori power analysis: helps determine the statistical power needed in order to detect relationships in the data.

bar graphs: also known as simple bar charts, a common way of visually presenting categorical (nominal, ordinal, and dichotomous) data.

between-group degrees of freedom: the calculation of degrees of freedom made comparing groups in ANOVA (number of groups – 1).

between-group sum of squares: a comparison of the individual group means to the grand mean in ANOVA. The squared difference between the grand mean and the group mean is multiplied by the group n. The numbers are summed, and the resulting number is the between-group sum of squares.

bimodal distribution: when there are two peaks (modes) in a distribution.

bivariate regression: refers to an Ordinary Least Squares (OLS) method regression for two variables: one independent variable (the predictor) and one dependent variable (the variable you wish to predict).

boxplots: useful visual tools to present measures of central tendency and variability (also known as box-and-whisker plots).

categorical variables: variables based on a series of categories that do not have meaningful numbers/values associated with them.

causal relationship: one where the independent variable *causes* a change in the dependent variable.

cells: the intersection of a row and a column in a crosstabulation.

census: data collection from each subject in a population, like the U.S. Census that is done every 10 years in the United States.

central limit theorem: the sampling distribution of the mean will approach a normal distribution if the sample size is large enough.

chi-square critical value: the obtained value in calculating the chi-square test of independence.

chi-square distribution: the distribution used to conduct a chi-square test of independence.

chi-square test of independence (χ^2): a nonparametric test to explore the relationship between two categorical variables.

clustered bar graphs: a graph where the bars of two or more different variables are placed next to another.

cluster sampling: a useful strategy when a sampling frame (a complete list of respondents) is not available.

codebook: a document that contains information about the variables in a dataset, typically including, but not limited to, data origin (e.g., survey question used to collect data), variable label, value labels, level of measurement, and missing values.

coefficient of determination (r^2): a PRE statistic for use with interval and ratio (continuous, scale) variables.

Cohen's *d*: a common effect size provided for a *t* test, which is equal to the number of standard deviations of difference between the two groups being studied.

cohort (longitudinal) research design: a design that resembles the repeated cross-sectional design, but adds a requirement for the members who are to be selected into the sample: they must have some common starting point. Typical cohorts include birth cohorts (born in the same year) and graduation cohorts (graduated from high school or college in the same year).

column margins: at the bottom of a crosstabulation, the sum of the values in the columns of the table.

column percentages: the percentage in each cell of the column calculated by taking the cell frequency divided by the column total.

columns: the vertical groups of cells in a crosstabulation.

conceptualization: the meaning or conceptual definition of a specific construct that a researcher proposes for his or her study.

concurrent validity: when a measurement is determined to correlate with other theoretically relevant measures in the study.

confidence interval: the interval within which the researcher believes the population parameter will fall. The likelihood, expressed as a percentage or a probability, that a specified interval will contain a population parameter is known as the confidence level.

construct validity: when an instrument is truly measuring the construct under study and not some other construct.

content validity: when all components of the construct are being measured. In order to be high in content validity, a measurement must assess the concept under study in a comprehensive way.

contingency tables: frequencies and/or percentages of one variable tabulated separately across different categories of a second variable. (Layers can be included to add a third variable.)

continuous quantitative variable: a variable having an infinite number of possible values between two units.

convenience sampling: sampling done entirely at the convenience of the researcher. As you might imagine, this type of sampling is the least useful since it is neither systematic nor random.

correlated: a relationship detected by Pearson's correlation coefficient (r).

correlational studies: see **correlated**.

Cramér's V: provides a measure of effect size for tables with more than two groups on one or both variables (i.e., nondichotomous categorical variables).

criterion-based validity: when a measurement correlates with other measures or outcomes.

critical value: where the nonrejection region of a distribution ends and the region of rejection begins for different degrees of freedom (distributions) and levels of alpha.

Cronbach's alpha: a statistical summary measure of the internal consistency of data collected across multiple items that form a scale. While there are no hard-and-fast rules regarding interpretation of Cronbach's alpha, the higher the value of Cronbach's alpha, the more consistent the items.

cross-sectional research: research in which the data are collected at one point in time. The data (observations) should represent a cross-section, or representative slice, of the population you intend to study.

cumulative frequencies: an additive summary of frequencies up to and including a given category.

cumulative frequency polygons: graphs that chart frequencies across multiple categories that also include *all preceding frequencies* (a running total).

cumulative percentages: a summary of accumulated percentages (the percentage with a given attribute plus all of the preceding attributes).

cumulative property of levels of measurement: a property that states that variables measured at higher levels can be treated as if they were measured at lower levels.

deductive research: research that begins with a theory and a hypothesis. The researcher proposes a hypothesis and at least one competing hypothesis (usually the statement of no difference), and then collects data (observations) to conduct the hypothesis test.

degrees of freedom: the number of cells that can vary based on the row and column totals.

dependent variable (DV): a variable that is influenced by one or more other (independent) variables.

dichotomous variables: variables having exactly two response categories or attributes.

difference between means: the absolute value obtained by subtracting one sample mean from another sample mean.

directional alternative hypothesis: a hypothesis that differs from the null hypothesis in that it states the outcome will be either "greater than" or "less than" across categories of a variable; also, a one-tailed hypothesis.

discrete quantitative variable: a variable that can take on only fixed values that are integers.

disproportionate stratified sampling: sampling in which the size of the sample drawn from each subgroup is disproportional to the size of that subgroup in the population.

distorted scaling: improper scales on one or more axes of a graph that misrepresent a distribution or relationship.

double-blind experiment: an experiment in which the experimenter does not know who is in the experimental or control groups.

dummy variable: a variable with two attributes: 0 and 1; 0 indicates absence of a characteristic, and 1 indicates its presence.

effect size: helps researchers determine whether results are *meaningful*. While statistical significance reveals how precise we are in our interpretation of an effect, effect size adds the magnitude of that effect. Both are necessary in order to accurately interpret the results of scientific research.

epsilon squared (ε^2): an effect size that corrects for sample size differences and the number of categories in the independent variable.

estimated standard error: a value used to represent the standard error by using the standard deviation of a sample in its computation rather than the standard deviation of a population (which is generally not known).

eta squared (η²): an effect size coefficient to determine the strength of mean differences across multiple groups.

excess kurtosis: kurtosis relative to the normal distribution.

exhaustive: used to describe a comprehensive list of the attributes or categories that comprise a variable.

expected frequencies: the frequencies of crosstabulated categories whose calculation is based on the assumption that there is no relationship between the independent and dependent variables.

experimental mortality: when people leave an experiment. Individuals can leave an experiment for a number of reasons (e.g., death, boredom, or moral disagreement with the subject matter). At best, this can limit the sample size; at worst, it can lead to selection bias.

experimenter bias: when the person running an experiment already knows who is in the experimental and control groups and then, perhaps unconsciously, treats them differently.

external validity: points to whether or not the results of a given study are applicable to other groups and contexts (generalizability).

face validity: a superficial assessment of whether or not the measurement "looks good at face value."

fail to reject the null hypothesis: a statement of no difference, or of no discernable relationship, between the variables of interest.

fixed sample panel research design: a research design that starts just like a repeated cross-sectional design, with a cross-section at Time 1. However, any similarities with the former longitudinal design end there. At Time 2, the researcher must follow up with the same group selected for this original sample at Time 1. Because the fixed sample panel design requires follow-up with the same respondents at a future point in time, the selection process is usually attuned to this so that you will have a better chance of having respondents follow up. Also, it is important to disclose to subjects that the nature of the study necessitates continuing data collection in the future and they will be contacted again.

frequency tables: summary tables that indicate how observed scores are distributed across a sample or population.

F statistic: the ratio of between-groups mean square and within-groups mean square.

full percentage: includes all cases in the denominator, even those with missing values.

gamma: a symmetrical measure of association for ordinal and dichotomous nominal variables.

General Social Survey (GSS): a national sample of Americans' opinions, attitudes, and lifestyles. According to the National Opinion Research Center, which administers the GSS, with the exception of the U.S. Census, the GSS is the most frequently analyzed source of information in the social sciences.

Glass's delta: a measure of effect size.

grand mean: the mean of the means of samples or subgroups.

grouped frequencies: a frequency distribution that combines some values together rather than presenting each value by itself.

Hedge's *g*: a measure of effect size.

history effect: if something important happens before the test is over.

homogeneity of variance: assumes that variances are equal among the populations being examined.

hypothesis: a testable statement about the relationship between two or more variables.

independent: a description indicating that two variables are unrelated and operate independently of each other.

independent samples *t* test: a procedure used to assess whether or not a mean significantly differs between two independent groups.

independent variable (IV): a variable that influences, or leads to some change or outcome in, another variable (dependent variable).

index: a measurement that is built on individual, real-world indicators of a social construct.

index of qualitative variation (IQV): a measure of variability for nominal variables; it is the ratio of the total number of differences in the distribution to the maximum number of possible differences that could have theoretically occurred in that distribution.

inductive research: research that begins with the observations (data that have already been collected, or perhaps are collected first for the purpose of the research). While not exclusively, inductive research tends to be more descriptive and qualitative, with a focus on studying observations for trends, patterns, or irregularities.

instrumentation bias: bias that occurs when a researcher chooses to use a *different* posttest measurement, instead of the same test as the pretest.

intended (target) population: the collection of people, things, places, or other units to which the research is intended to generalize.

internal consistency: the degree to which multiple items in a scale are consistent.

internal validity: a concept used widely within experimental research to assert the legitimacy of a causal relationship between a dependent and an independent variable.

interquartile range (IQR): a measure of variation for interval-ratio variables that indicates the width of the middle 50 percent of a distribution.

interval variable: a quantitative variable with a zero point that is arbitrary. In other words, a zero does not necessarily imply the absence of the construct.

Kendall's tau-*b*: an asymmetrical measure of association for ordinal and dichotomous nominal variables.

kurtosis: an indication of how concentrated the scores are around a measure of central tendency.

lambda: an asymmetrical measure of association for nominal variables.

leaves: the right portion of a stem and leaf plot.

leptokurtic distribution: kurtosis indicating that the distribution has a pointier peak and steeper curve in the shoulders of the distribution than a typical normal (mesokurtic) distribution.

Likert-type items: items in which individuals choose from a range of possible responses that reflect their feelings, knowledge, or attitudes.

linear: a statistical test or prediction that is modeled upon a straight line.

line graph: a scatterplot where a line is drawn across the plot such that its slope can change at each value across the variable along the *x*-axis (independent variable).

logistic regression (or logit regression analysis): a type of regression analysis performed on a dichotomous dependent variable and one or more dichotomous independent variables.

longitudinal research: research that relies upon the collection of data at more than one point (or interval) in time.

lower bound: the smallest value beneath which the interval ceases to extend.

lower tail: the tail of a curve to the left of (below) the mean.

margins: refers to column and row marginals in a crosstabulation.

maturation effect: when people mature between the time the experiment begins and the time it ends.

mean: the arithmetic average of a distribution and an appropriate measure of central tendency for an interval-ratio distribution that is not skewed.

measurement validity: when the researcher has actually measured what was intended to be measured.

median: the case or respondent in the distribution below which 50% of the distribution falls. Therefore, the median is truly the middle score.

mesokurtic distribution: the kurtosis of a normal distribution.

mode: the category or attribute with the largest frequency.

modified boxplot: signals outliers in the extremes of the distribution; the outliers are represented outside of the pattern of the data with symbols.

multimodal distribution: when there are more than two peaks (modes) in a distribution.

multivariate regression: a type of OLS regression analysis that involves two or more independent variables (predictors) and one dependent variable.

mutually exclusive: an indication that there is no overlap in categories.

negatively skewed: refers to a distribution that appears to be pulled to the left (negative) side; this is a representation of a distribution that has outliers on the left (negative side) that pull the mean to a value lower than that of the median.

negative relationship: a relationship where as the independent variable increases, the dependent variable decreases (and/or as the independent variable decreases, the dependent variable increases).

nominal variables: variables composed of a list of different categories that cannot be rank ordered in any way. They are used to describe membership in mutually exclusive categories, but aside from assignment into a particular group, nominal variables have no other measurable properties.

nondirectional: a relationship where one or more of the variables are nominal/categorical.

nondirectional alternative hypothesis: a hypothesis that differs from the null hypothesis in that it states the outcomes will be "not equal"; also, a two-tailed hypothesis.

nonparametric tests: tests that do not use sample data to approximate a larger sample (also known as distribution-free statistics).

nonprobability sample: when the probability of members of the intended (target) population being selected into the sample is not known.

nonrejection region: the area under the curve where the null hypothesis would not be rejected.

normal quantile-quantile plot: a visualization of how the distribution of scores for a variable compares to what one would expect in a normal distribution (also known as a normal probability plot or a Q-Q plot).

null hypothesis (H_0): a hypothesis that suggests that a relationship, change, or effect *does not appear to exist* between the study's variables. In other words, the independent variable does not exert a substantial influence on the dependent variable.

observed frequencies: values obtained from the collected data.

obtained t statistic: the value of t calculated in a t test.

obtained value: the calculated value in a statistical test.

OLS regression (linear regression): a type of regression analysis that minimizes the sum of all the squared distances from each observed data point to the prediction line. Since the prediction equation will result in a straight line when graphed on a Cartesian plane (*x-y* coordinate axis), this type of analysis is sometimes also called linear regression.

omega squared (ω^2): an effect size that corrects for sample size differences and the number of categories in the independent variable.

one-tailed test: a directional hypothesis test that takes into account area at one end of the distribution.

operationalization: a description of how the researcher empirically measures or observes the construct.

ordinal variable: a variable with categories that specify a specific characteristic of an individual or individuals *but can be rank ordered*, thereby giving information about an individual's placement relative to others on the scale.

outlier: a value that is significantly outside the interval of the rest of the scores in the distribution.

parametric tests: procedures where information about a sample is used to estimate the population characteristics.

peak: the highest point of a distribution.

Pearson's *r* (correlation coefficient): a statistic calculated to determine if two interval-ratio variables vary together.

percentages: a representation of the proportion of a value divided by the total sample or population size.

percentile ranks: a value that exhibits the percentage of the population above which the subject ranks.

periodicity: when the sequence of respondents or other elements (list, physical structure) varies in a regular pattern. If there is a regular pattern among the list of elements and the value of *N* used in systematic random sampling causes some types of elements to be selected more than others, this creates a situation where, indeed, the sample is not random at all.

phi coefficient of effect size: a measure of effect size.

pie chart: a graph that visually illustrates the relative frequency or percentage of each category in its relation to the whole sample.

platykurtic distribution: a kurtosis flatter than a typical normal (mesokurtic) distribution.

plot legend: in a stem and leaf plot, a description of how to transform the stem in order to interpret the data.

positively skewed: refers to a distribution that appears to be pulled to the right (positive) side; this is a representation of a distribution that has outliers on the right (positive side) that pull the mean to a value higher than that of the median.

positive relationship: a relationship where as the independent variable increases, the dependent variable also increases (and/or as the independent variable decreases, the dependent variable decreases).

post hoc tests: in the event that the null hypothesis is rejected, additional procedures that can help you discern the effects of individual pairs.

predictive validity: when a measure corresponds to some theoretically relevant pre-established criterion.

probability sample: when it is known in advance, the probability of any member of the intended (target) population to be selected into the sample.

proportional reduction in error (PRE) statistics: statistics that allow us to determine the proportional reduction of error achieved by adding one or more variables to an analysis (even if it is the initial independent variable).

proportionate stratified sampling: when the size of the sample drawn from each subgroup is proportional to the size of that particular subgroup in the population.

p value: the probability that a relationship exists by chance.

quantitative variable: the highest level of measurement for variables, having meaningful numbers associated with them referring to specific quantities.

quota sampling: the nonprobability sampling method counterpart to stratified random sampling. It works in much the same way, except, of course, that a quota sample is not random, not a probability sample.

range: a measure of variation for interval-ratio variables. To compute the range, take the difference between the highest (maximum) and the lowest (minimum) scores in the distribution.

ratio variable: a quantitative variable that has a meaningful zero point, whereby a zero indicates that there is a complete absence of that variable.

region of rejection: the area under the curve where the null hypothesis would be rejected.

regression: a statistical tool that allows you to estimate/predict outcomes for interval and ratio (scale, continuous) variables.

reject the null hypothesis: a statement indicating that there exists a sufficient likelihood that the null hypothesis is false.

relative frequencies: frequencies that provide a proportional measure of each category relative to the total sample.

reliability: the ability to yield the same results with the same instrument after repeated measurement.

repeated cross-sectional research design: a research design in which a cross-section is taken at Time 1, then another independent cross-section of the same population is taken at Time 2. If the design calls for it, additional independent cross-sections can be taken at Time 3, Time 4, and so on, as many times as prescribed. Sampling methods used in each of the time periods should be the same or similar, unless you have documented evidence of improved sampling over time and you can demonstrate that the sample taken at each point in time is representative of the target population.

respondent-driven sampling: a sophisticated improvement on snowball sampling. If done properly, this method affords the researchers using it greater ability to generalize than standard snowball sampling does. Improvements over snowball sampling begin with the introduction of incentives to improve the representativeness of the sample.

row margins: at the right side of a crosstabulation, the sum of the values in the rows of the table.

row percentages: the percentage in each cell of the row calculated by taking the cell frequency divided by the row total.

rows: the horizontal groups of cells in a crosstabulation.

scale: a composite measure that is based on multiple measures of a latent construct.

scatterplots: graphs that present the relationship between two interval-ratio variables. The data are encoded, or plotted, simultaneously on the x-axis (independent variable) and y-axis (dependent variable) in order to illustrate how two variables are related.

selection bias: when the experimental and control groups differ along some important characteristic related to the study.

selectivity: the likelihood of failing to reject the null hypothesis among data that comply with the null hypothesis (i.e., correctly failing to reject the null hypothesis).

simple random sample: selecting each case solely on the basis of chance, where all cases have an equal chance of being selected into the sample. You can roll dice, flip a coin, pick numbers out of a hat, or use some other purely chance-driven method to select each case for the sample.

skewness: when a distribution has a few extreme scores on only one side.

snowball sampling: a method of nonprobability sampling that is useful for sampling hard-to-reach populations. Snowball sampling is sometimes also called chain sampling or chain referral. The essential component of snowball sampling is that respondents refer the researcher to other respondents who meet the parameters of the intended (target) population. Those referred respondents refer others, and so on.

Somers' d: an asymmetrical measure of association for ordinal and dichotomous nominal variables.

split ballot design: a survey research design that allows data from more variables to be collected by splitting the sample into subsections (ballots) and asking some questions of members of only one ballot. This reduces the inevitable survey fatigue that may invalidate the survey if too many questions were continuously asked of each person.

split-test reliability: a type of reliability that groups similar items in a measurement instrument into two sets of equivalent items that are split into two halves. The scores from each half are compared to determine the degree of correlation between them. Correlation should be high among questions reliably measuring the same concept.

stacked bar chart (also stacked bar graph): a graph where bars of different variables are stacked one on another.

stacked bar graph: see **stacked bar chart**.

standard deviation: a measure of variation for interval-ratio variables. It is calculated by taking the square root of the variance (i.e., taking the square root of the average of the squared deviations from the mean of the distribution).

standard error: the standard deviation of a sampling distribution of sample means.

statistically significant: refers to a relationship between two or more variables that is caused by something other than chance.

statistical power: an indication of the ability of a test to produce an accurate result if a researcher rejects the null hypothesis.

statistical regression toward the mean: a statistical phenomenon where data that are either extremely higher or extremely lower than the mean are likely to be closer to the mean in another measurement at a second time interval.

stem: the left (root) part of a stem and leaf plot.

stem and leaf plots: a way of presenting a large group of numbers in categories based on their units. In a stem and leaf plot, the values are presented from the lowest to the highest score and are separated into two parts: the stem and the leaves. The stem represents the first digit or digits of the number, which are usually displayed on the left side of the plot. The leaves are commonly presented to the right of the stem and consist of the last digit or digits that correspond to the beginning digits represented by the stem. The plot legend describes how to transform the stem in order to interpret the data.

stratified random sampling: a method of sampling achieved by dividing the population into subgroups based on one or more variables that are related to the research question, then drawing a simple random (or perhaps systematic random) sample from each of the designated subgroups. A sample can be stratified by one or more variables.

symmetrical: refers to a distribution that is identical both above and below the middle.

systematic random sampling: a method of sampling where every Nth member in the total population is chosen for inclusion in the sample after the first member of the sample is selected at random from among the first N members of the population. N is the ratio computed by dividing the population size by the intended sample size.

tails: the area under the curve toward the edges of a distribution (left/negative and right/positive).

t **critical values:** the cut points designating statistical significance in a *t* test.

t **distribution:** the distribution that is used when conducting a *t* test.

temporal precedence: one of the criteria that must be established for the independent variable; that is, the independent variable (cause) must occur *before* the dependent variable (effect) in time.

testing effect: when a participant in an experiment knows the answers to posttest questions because he or she was asked the same questions in the pretest.

test–retest reliability: an assessment of a measurement's reliability based on the consistency of results after repeated administration. Responses from measures taken at Time 1 and Time 2 are assessed to estimate the stability of the measure over the two time points. A reliable question should elicit a similar response from one administration to the next.

test statistic: the computed value of a statistical hypothesis test.

total sum of squares: the sum of the squared difference of each individual score in the sample from the grand mean. This number represents how individuals in the whole sample vary around the grand mean.

transformed: quantitative variables can be transformed into categorical variables— that is, we can take the information from a quantitative variable and make it into a variable with the characteristics of those variables with less information.

truncated graph: a graph whose axes (or one axis) does not extend to the full range of the data.

two-tailed test: a nondirectional hypothesis test that takes into account area at both ends of the distribution.

Type I error: when a researcher rejects the null hypothesis (states there is a relation-ship) but the null hypothesis is true (there is no relationship in real life). A Type I error is also referred to as a "false positive" since the data do show a relationship (positive) but this conclusion is false.

Type II error: when a researcher fails to reject the null hypothesis but the null hypothesis is, in fact, false. Type II errors are also known as "false negative" errors since the researcher *does not* find a relationship (negative) but that conclusion is false.

typology: a composite measure that uses discrete categories based on information from one or more variables.

unimodal: a distribution with a single mode.

upper bound: the largest value above which the interval ceases to extend.

upper tail: the tail of a distribution that is at the right (positive) side of the graph.

valid percentage: the percentage of the distribution with a given value based on a sample size that *excludes cases with missing values.*

variability: the amount of variation in individuals' scores for a given variable.

variable: a logical grouping of attributes that can be observed and measured and is expected to vary from person to person in a population.

variance: a measure of variation for interval-ratio variables. The variance is computed by taking the average of the squared deviations from the mean of the distribution.

whiskers: the end lines (tails) that extend beyond the box of a box and whisker plot.

within-group degrees of freedom: the calculation of degrees of freedom made in ANOVA $(N - g)$.

within-group sum of squares: the squared difference of each individual from the individual group's mean (ANOVA).

z score (standard score): a value that denotes how many standard deviations away from the mean a particular raw score lies. A positive (+) z score is an indicator of a raw score that is greater than the mean. A negative (–) z score is an indicator of a raw score that is lower than the mean.

• About the Authors •

William E. Wagner, III, PhD, holds a joint appointment as Professor of Sociology and Health Sciences at California State University, Channel Islands. Prior to coming to CSU Channel Islands, Dr. Wagner served as a member of the faculty and Director of the Institute for Social and Community Research at California State University, Bakersfield. He completed his PhD in sociology at the University of Illinois, Chicago. Dr. Wagner also holds undergraduate degrees in mathematics as well as anthropology/sociology from St. Mary's College of Maryland, as well as an MPH degree (Master of Public Health) from California State University, Northridge. He has published in national and regional scholarly journals on topics such as urban sociology, homophobia, academic status, sports, and public health. Dr. Wagner is author of *Using SPSS Statistics for Research Methods and Social Science Statistics* (6th edition, 2016), a coauthor (with Earl Babbie and Jeanne Zaino) of the ninth edition of *Adventures in Social Research* (2015), and a coauthor (with Erin Ruel and Brian Gillespie) of *The Practice of Survey Research: Theory and Application* (2015).

Brian Joseph Gillespie, PhD, is author of *Household Mobility in America: Patterns, Processes, and Outcomes* (Palgrave Macmillan, 2017) and coauthor of *The Practice of Survey Research: Theory and Applications* (SAGE, 2016). He has also authored or coauthored more than 20 peer-reviewed articles on topics related to migration, families, and interpersonal relationships using both quantitative and qualitative methods. He is currently Assistant Professor of Sociology at Sonoma State University, where he teaches courses on demography, research methods, and statistics.